T0055304

The Art of SERIES

EDITED BY CHARLES BAXTER

The Art of series is a line of books reinvigorating the practice of craft and criticism. Each book is a brief, witty, and useful exploration of fiction, nonfiction, or poetry by a writer impassioned by a singular craft issue. *The Art of* volumes provide a series of sustained examinations of key, but sometimes neglected, aspects of creative writing by some of contemporary literature's finest practitioners.

THE ART OF THE
POETIC LINE

Also by James Longenbach

The Art of the

POETIC LINE

James Longenbach

Graywolf Press

Publication of this volume is made possible in part by a grant provided by the Minnesota State Arts Board, through an appropriation by the Minnesota State Legislature; a grant from the Wells Fargo Foundation Minnesota; and a grant from the National Endowment for the Arts, which believes that a great nation deserves great art. Significant support has also been provided by the Bush Foundation; Target; the McKnight Foundation; and other generous contributions from foundations, corporations, and individuals. To these organizations and individuals we offer our heartfelt thanks.

Clara Ueland and Walt McCarthy are pleased to support the Graywolf Press *Art of* series in honor of Brenda Ueland.

Published by Graywolf Press
212 Third Avenue North, Suite 485
Minneapolis, Minnesota 55401
All rights reserved.

www.graywolfpress.org

Published in the United States of America

ISBN 978-1-55597-488-6

10 12 14 15 13 11 9

Library of Congress Control Number: 2007924773

Series cover design: Scott Sorenson

Cover art: Scott Sorenson

The meaning of a poem is in the cadences and the shape of the lines and the pulse of the thought which is given by those lines.

—George Oppen

Contents

Preface

Poetry is the sound of language organized in lines. More than meter, more than rhyme, more than images or alliteration or figurative language, line is what distinguishes our experience of poetry as poetry, rather than some other kind of writing. Great prose might be filled with metaphors. The rhythmic vitality of prose might be so intense that it rises to moments of regularity we can scan. Its diction may be more sensuous, more evocative, than that of many poems. We wouldn't be attracted to the notion of prose poetry if it didn't feel exciting to abandon the decorum of lines.

But while line is central to our experience of poetry, it is notoriously difficult to talk about—much more difficult than meter, rhyme, or syntax, even though our experience of all of these poetic elements is bound up with our experience of line. What's more, line has no identity except in relation to other elements in the poem, especially the syntax of the poem's sentences. It is not an abstract concept, and its qualities cannot be described generally or schematically. It cannot be associated reliably with the way we speak or breathe. Nor can its function be understood merely from its visual appearance on the page. The line's function is sonic, a way of organizing the sound of language, and only by listening to the effect of a particular line in the context of a particular poem can we come to understand how line works.

This book does not presume any long-standing familiarity with the practice of lineation. It examines metered lines, rhymed lines, syllabic lines, and a variety of free-verse lines. Along the way, it employs only a handful of familiar terms while introducing a smaller handful of new ones. Most prominently, it rejects the term "line break" as an inaccurate metaphor, preferring the term "line ending": at the point where the line ends, syntax may or may not be broken, continuing in the next line. This is another way of saying that line cannot be understood by describing the line alone: the music of a poem—no matter if metered, syllabic, or free—depends on what the syntax is doing when the line ends.

The book's first chapter emphasizes this point. Surveying a variety of different kinds of lines, it shows how the power of lineation arises from the relationship between the lines and the syntax of a particular poem. The second chapter examines the different ways in which lines may end, demonstrating that the power especially of free-verse lineation depends on the interaction of different kinds of line endings within the same poem. The third chapter discusses the relationship of lineated poems to prose, not only examining different kinds of prose poetry but suggesting that the very power of line asks us to wonder how it would feel to do without line.

I have tried to be descriptive, not proscriptive. Since no two lines function in exactly the same way, I offer a wide range of examples—from John Ashbery and Louise Glück to William Shakespeare and John Milton. If you find in these pages a poet who helps you to hear the work of line, read lots of poems by that poet. But if a poet I have not treated suddenly seems crucial to you, read that poet instead. On every page of this book is something I have learned by listening to others.

THE ART OF THE
POETIC LINE

Line and Syntax

Whatever else he is, Shakespeare is one of the great prose writers in the English language.

> Beneath is all the fiend's. There's hell, there's darkness, there is the sulphurous pit, burning, scalding, stench, consumption. Fie, fie, fie; pah, pah! Give me an ounce of civet, good apothecary, sweeten my imagination.

This is King Lear's madness speaking. While the syntax holds steady in the second sentence ("there's ... there's"), the diction leaps from elaborate Latinate words (sulphurous, consumption) to the most basic Anglo-Saxon words (pit, stench). A list gives way to repeated exclamation, pure sound: pah, pah. Then the disparities in diction take control of the logic: civet, apothecary, sweeten, imagination. The roaring prophet who begins this speech is in no time superseded by a courtier in search of a fine perfume.

Shakespeare's sentences have many of the qualities we associate with the texture of great poetry (patterned syntax, varied diction, metaphorical implication, disjunctive movement), but they are not set in lines—at least they are not set in lines in one of the two earliest printings of *King*

Lear. In the other printing, however, these sentences are set in lines. A few of the words are different, but the basic shape of the sentences remains the same.

> Beneath is all the fiend's. There's hell, there's darkness,
> There's the sulphury pit, burning, scalding,
> Stench, consummation. Fie, fie, fie; pah, pah!
> Give me an ounce of civet, good apothecary,
> To sweeten my imagination.

We don't know what Shakespeare intended. One compositor set this passage as prose, the other set it as poetry; they may have been working from different manuscripts, neither of which was necessarily Shakespeare's own. How does the division of these four sentences into four and a half lines change our apprehension of them? What procedure determines the length of the line? Does that procedure introduce arbitrary line endings, or are the line endings functional in their own right?

In this chapter I will discuss metrical lines (which follow a pattern of stressed and unstressed syllables), syllabic lines (which adhere to a fixed number of syllables, whether stressed or unstressed), and free-verse lines (in which the relationship between stressed and unstressed syllables is consistently various). In every case, however the line is shaped, what will matter is not the line as such but the relationship of the line to the poem's syntax—to the unfolding structure of the poem's sentences. That relationship is endlessly various. Short lines or long lines don't inevitably function in any particular way. A rhyming line doesn't necessarily function differently from a free-verse line. In the end, line doesn't exist as a principle in itself. Line has a meaningful identity only when we begin to hear its relationship to other elements in the poem.

Shakespeare's lines are organized metrically. While his plays often contain passages of prose, the language of his plays is most often cast in blank verse: unrhymed iambic pentameter lines. That is, unrhymed lines in which there are usually five pairs of syllables: the second syllable of each pair gets more stress than the first syllable.

> BeNEATH is ALL the FIEND'S. There's HELL, there's
>   DARKness

None of the lines in the passage I've quoted from *King Lear* is a perfect pentameter: although it contains five stressed syllables, this line has an extra unstressed syllable hanging on to its end. The second line is missing an unstressed syllable at its beginning. And the third line scans programmatically only if we stress the syllables in an unnatural way.

> Stench, CONsumMAtion, FIE, fie, FIE; pah, PAH!

No actor would say the line this way, if only because he would not give all the stressed syllables an equal amount of stress. As in all accomplished poetry, there is a tension here between pattern and variation. If we've heard a lot of iambic pentameter lines before encountering these ones, we will feel this tension as pleasure.

Counting the stresses helps us to recognize a principle that divides Shakespeare's prose sentences into lines, but merely counting the stresses won't let us understand the function of line. That's because I've so far described the line only as an arbitrary unit: something that might contain a certain pattern of stressed and unstressed syllables. Now we need to listen to the way in which this unit, this way of organizing the syllables, plays against the syntax of the sentences. Listen to the whole of King Lear's speech, paying attention to the varied length of the sentences in relationship to the relatively consistent length of the lines.

When I do stare, see how the subject quakes!
I pardon that man's life. What was thy cause?
Adultery? Thou shalt not die. Die for adultery!
No, the wren goes to't, and the small gilded fly
Does lecher in my sight.
Let copulation thrive, for Gloucester's bastard son
Was kinder to his father than my daughters

Got 'tween the lawful sheets. To't, luxury, pell-mell,
For I lack soldiers. Behold yon simp'ring dame,
Whose face between her forks presageth snow,
That minces virtue, and does shake the head
To hear of pleasure's name:
The fitchew nor the soiled horse goes to't
With a more riotous appetite. Down from the waist
They're centaurs, though women all above.
But to the girdle do the gods inherit;
Beneath is all the fiend's. There's hell, there's darkness,
There's the sulphury pit, burning, scalding,
Stench, consummation. Fie, fie, fie; pah, pah!
Give me an ounce of civet, good apothecary,
To sweeten my imagination.

This speech is made of twenty-one lines, most of which are pentameters. The speech is also made of fifteen sentences. What is the relationship between these sentences and these lines? How does that relationship help to make us hear the unfolding of the speech in one way rather than another?

First, we may notice that the sentence and the line are not the same thing: sometimes a single sentence may take up a single line, but often the sentence is either shorter than the line or longer than the line. Second, we may notice that even though sentence and line are not the same thing, there is no regular relation-ship between the sentences and the lines; the sentences do not exceed or fall short of the line in any predict-able way. Third, we notice that the lines end differently. Some lines end with a full stop—a period, a ques-tion mark, or an exclamation point. Others end with a comma, a semicolon, or a colon that joins together two clauses or phrases within a sentence. And others end with no punctuation at all: the syntax continues in the next line. We might be tempted to say that the line "breaks" at such a moment, but the line merely ends—it doesn't break. Rather than thinking about what often gets called "line breaks," it's more helpful to think about "line endings": the syntax may or may not break at the point where the line ends.

The opening line of the passage is made of one com-plete syntactical unit: the syntax does not break. The homeless, bedraggled Lear is clinging pathetically to his lost power, and the opening line feels like a declaration.

When I do stare, see how the subject quakes!

The second line is also syntactically complete, but it is made of two sentences, a statement and a question.

I pardon that man's life. What was thy cause?

Then the third line, also syntactically complete, is made of three units: a question, a statement, and an exclamation.

Adultery? Thou shalt not die. Die for adultery!

Though we move from one to two to three syntactical units within these lines, all three lines are end-stopped: syntax ends where the line ends. What is the effect of three such lines in a row?

King Lear is blinded by madness here. He imagines that his friend Gloucester is merely an adulterer who has come before him for mercy, when in fact Gloucester has literally been blinded by the husband of one of Lear's daughters. The relationship of the lines to the syntax does not make Lear sound mad, however: the lines organize the syntax in a way that feels balanced and coherent. Any actor reciting this passage would be led by the relationship of the syntax and the lines to read this passage with a strong sense of reasonableness: the opening declaration (in which syntax equals line) is superseded by lines that are divided logically into two and then three syntactical units. The sound of logical thought is not inappropriate here, for there is a strange logic to what Lear says. Gloucester is indeed an adulterer, and he has been unable to distinguish his loyal legitimate son from his disloyal bastard son.

What happens to the relationship of line to syntax as the speech progresses?

> No, the wren goes to't, and the small gilded fly
> Does lecher in my sight.
> Let copulation thrive, for Gloucester's bastard son
> Was kinder to his father than my daughters
> Got 'tween the lawful sheets.

Here we have two sentences, the first of which takes up two lines, the second of which takes up two and a half lines. For the first time in the passage, syntax has exceeded the end of the line, spilling into the following line. We say that such lines are "enjambed," the word "enjambment" referring generally to lines that end while the syntax keeps going. What is the effect of these kinds of lines, following on the three end-stopped lines preceding them?

First, the mere fact that these sentences are longer than the ones preceding them makes us feel that Lear's mind is in motion, launched from the runway of the three end-stopped lines. Second, the fact that both these sentences are enjambed or broken across the line introduces a formal tension to the sentences, one that is completely lacking in the first three end-stopped lines.

Consider the effect of the first longer sentence if it were written this way.

> No, the wren goes to't. And the small gilded fly.
> They lecher in my sight.

Had Shakespeare broken up the sentence, he would have continued with the sonic decorum established by the three opening lines of the speech, in which sentences are short and always end where the line ends: the sound of coherence would prevail. Instead, we move in these lines to a new sound—the excitement of syntax overriding the line to which it had previously been subservient. It's important to recognize that no particular kind of line has any inevitable relationship to sound or sense; that is, an enjambment does not necessarily speed up the line or contribute to a sense of frantic movement in thought. But in this speech, we feel Lear's rabid enthusiasm for his own thought increasing as the speech unfolds, moving from one kind of relationship between syntax and line to another relationship. This progression is appropriate, since the impression of logic is disintegrating as Lear speaks: we know, though Lear does not, that Gloucester's bastard son was not kind to his father.

The disintegration continues as Lear begins to rail at what seems to him the essentially lascivious nature of female sexuality.

> Behold yon simp'ring dame,
> Whose face between her forks presageth snow,
> That minces virtue, and does shake the head
> To hear of pleasure's name:
> The fitchew nor the soiled horse goes to't
> With a more riotous appetite.

Even if we don't follow Lear's sense here, we hear the rising passion of his voice because of the increasing tension between syntax and line within the longer sentences. Again, the lines offer implicit instructions to the actor: having begun by reinforcing the impression of reasonableness, the speech should devolve into an increasingly questionable passion. Blaming women will get Lear nowhere.

How, then, do the final lines of this speech, the lines with which I began, sound after we've listened to this movement from an initial trio of end-stopped lines to a group of mostly enjambed lines?

> Beneath is all the fiend's. There's hell, there's
>   darkness,
> There's the sulphury pit, burning, scalding,
> Stench, consummation. Fie, fie, fie; pah, pah!
> Give me an ounce of civet, good apothecary,
> To sweeten my imagination.

Here, at the end of the speech, we return to end-stopped lines. Unlike the trio of opening lines, these lines don't all end with a full stop, but the lines are not enjambed: some definitive turn of syntax takes place at the moment when the line ends. The result is that we feel we have returned to a sonic decorum similar to the one with which we began. The speech begins firmly, determinedly; then it grows into an enthusiasm fueled by Lear's madness; finally it calms down again.

The opening and concluding lines have a different effect, however, for while the concluding lines may *sound* like a return to sanity, they are in fact the most wildly associative lines in the speech: Lear is still talking about the female body when he says "beneath is all the fiend's." Formally, the speech moves from the initial order of syntax matching line through the excitement of syntax exceeding line, ultimately returning to the initial terms of order. But thematically, the speech moves inexorably toward increasingly disordered thought. The fluctuating tension between syntax and line is itself in tension with the thematic content of the speech, and there is no predictable relationship between the form and the content. In other words, the passage does not simply describe a movement of thought; it embodies and complicates that movement through the relationship of syntax and line. This is what great poems do.

The lines I've examined so far are of course taken from a play written in verse, not from a poem as such: I've begun my discussion with dramatic poetry so that I might speak freely of the passage as something we hear. It's a commonplace to talk about the speaker of any poem, but the notion of a speaker may or may not be useful; a poem might feel more like a concatenation of various linguistic strands than like the utterance of a single person. In any case, however, the sonic properties of the poem's language are always crucial. When a poet creates a relationship between the syntax and the lines of her poems, she is trying to organize the language on the page so that it corresponds to what she hears in her head. The poet may speak the lines out loud while composing the poem, but she generally does this to test what is on the page against what she hears—much as a composer turns to the piano not to discover the melody but to confirm it. Then, once the poem is finished, its sounds are re-created in the mind of the reader, and the relationship between line and syntax is one of the primary means through which this sonic information is transmitted. Reading a poem out loud helps us to hear that relationship, but poetry does not literally need to be spoken in order to exist primarily as a sonic work of art.

Listen to the first three stanzas of a little poem by William Carlos Williams. The syntax of the first line follows from the poem's title.

To a Poor Old Woman

munching a plum on
the street a paper bag
of them in her hand.

They taste good to her
They taste good
to her. They taste
good to her

You can see it by
the way she gives herself
to the one half
sucked out in her hand

By eschewing most punctuation, this poem puts
even more pressure on the relationship of syntax and
line to shape the pulse of thought. The poem's first sentence is made of run-on syntax; it is also heavily enjambed. As a result, when we come to the first line of
the second stanza—

They taste good to her

—we feel that the poem has reached a stable point after
the initial movement of the syntax through the lines.

But then Williams makes us think about the way we've heard this syntactically complete line. We hear the following line and a half differently because of the way the syntax is broken over the line ending.

>   They taste good
>   to her

And we hear the next line and a half differently as well.

>   They taste
>   good to her

The sentence has not changed, but the relationship of its syntax to the line has adjusted the way we hear the sentence's pattern of intonation and stress: because of the location of the enjambment, we hear the sentence first as "They taste GOOD to her" and then as "They TASTE good to her."

Williams is altering the sound of his sentence, but it's interesting to note that the next line of the poem is "you can see it": we have heard the syntax in a particular ways because it is arranged and rearranged on the page in a particular ways. We know a poem is divided into lines because of the visual arrangement on the page, but the function of the line is sonic. So when we come to the final lines of the poem—

Comforted
a solace of ripe plums
seeming to fill the air
They taste good to her

—we return to the same point of syntactical stability
we encountered in the first line of the second stanza:
"They taste good to her." But our sense of the line is
now enriched by the different ways in which this little
string of five monosyllabic words could be stressed. The
line looks the same, but we hear the line differently.

Williams's poem is written in free verse: that is,
rather than following a particular pattern of stressed
and unstressed syllables (as the iambic pentameter lines
of Shakespeare's blank verse more or less do), each line
has its own rhythmic identity. But just as there are many
kinds of metered verse, so are there different varieties of free verse. While Williams's poem depends, like
Shakespeare's, on the strategic interplay of enjambed
and end-stopped lines, Walt Whitman's free-verse lines
are almost never enjambed.

In vain the buzzard houses herself with the sky,
In vain the snake slides through the creepers and logs,
In vain the elk takes to the inner passes of the woods,
In vain the razor-bill'd auk sails far north to Labrador,
I follow quickly, I ascend to the nest in the fissure of
    the cliff.

Here, every line is a complete syntactical unit. The poem's energy derives not from the variable tension between line and syntax but from the variety of rhythmic patterns within the line, the different patterns playing off the steady beat of the repeated phrase that begins each line ("In vain").

Both Whitman and Williams are creating a particular relationship between line and syntax, and both poems depend, as all poems do, on the interplay of what changes with what stays the same—the simultaneous creation and disruption of pattern. But the differences between Whitman and Williams ought to feel as prominent as the similarities between Williams and Shakespeare: everything I've said about the fluctuating relationship of syntax and line in Williams's free verse applies equally well to Shakespeare's blank verse. Attention to the line tends to undermine a narrow preference for one or another form of poetry, for if you can hear what line is doing to your experience of the syntax in a free-verse poem, then you can hear what line is doing in a metered poem.

It's instructive to remember that blank verse once seemed as controversial as free verse seemed in the early years of the twentieth century. The earliest surviving poetry in the Western tradition is organized in lines. Tellingly, it was not always written down in lines, a fact that reminds us that line is ultimately a sonic rather than a visual element of the poem. As poetry began to be written in vernacular languages, the addition of rhyme to the line seemed to many people a barbarity. Then, by the seventeenth century, when Milton was writing *Paradise Lost* in blank verse, the deletion of rhyme from line seemed to some people equally barbarous. What does the addition of rhyme do to our sense of the line's relationship to syntax? In what way does rhyme alert us to the work that all lines, rhymed or unrhymed, metered or unmetered, end-stopped or enjambed, are performing in relationship to syntax?

The three stanzas of Donald Justice's "Nostalgia and Complaint of the Grandparents" end with the same sentence: "The dead don't get around much anymore." Like Williams, Justice lineates the refrain differently in each stanza, the shifting enjambment asking us to place additional stress on the syllable with which the line ends. This version of the sentence—

> The dead
> Don't get around much anymore

—sounds different from this version.

> The dead don't get around
> Much anymore.

Unlike Williams, however, Justice draws attention to his enjambments by marking the ends of the lines with rhyme. At the end of the penultimate line of the first stanza we emphasize the word "dead" not only because of the enjambment but because the syllable rhymes with "spread" in the line preceding it. The syntax urges us forward but the allure of similar sounds pulls us back.

> Our diaries squatted, toad-like,
> On dark closet ledges.
> Forget-me-not and thistle
> Decalcomaned the pages.
> But where, where are they now,
>   All the sad squalors
> Of those between-wars parlors?—
> Cut flowers; and the sunlight spilt like soda
>   On torporous rugs; the photo
>   Albums all outspread . . .
>   *The dead*
> *Don't get around much anymore.*

And at the end of the penultimate line of the second stanza we emphasize the word "get" because it rhymes with the word "set."

> There was an hour when daughters
> Practiced arpeggios;
> Their mothers, awkward and proud,
> Would listen, smoothing their hose—
> Sundays, half-past five!

Do you recall
How the sun used to loll,
Lazily, just beyond the roof,
Bloodshot and aloof?
We thought it would never set.
The dead don't get
Around much anymore.

And at the end of the third stanza we emphasize the second syllable of the word "around" because it rhymes with "ground."

Eternity resembles
One long Sunday afternoon.
No traffic passes; the cigar smoke
Curls in a blue cocoon.
Children, have you nothing
For our cold sakes?
No tea? No little tea cakes?
Sometimes now the rains disturb
Even our remote suburb.
There's a dampness underground.
The dead don't get around
Much anymore.

The impact of the shifting refrain depends on the fact that everything else about the stanza stays pretty much the same. In each case, the second and fourth lines rhyme ("afternoon" and "cocoon"), the sixth and seventh lines rhyme ("sakes" and "cakes"), and the eighth and ninth lines rhyme ("disturb" and "suburb"). But this complicated stanza form doesn't matter in itself, just as the fact that Shakespeare's iambic pentameter line has five stresses doesn't really matter in itself. What matters is the way in which the syntax of the poem's sentences moves through these lines of varying length. What matters is the way in which the rhymes make us especially aware of what is happening to the syntax at the ends of these lines. What matters is the way in which the consistent pattern of the stanza works against the variable grain of the sentences, forcing us to hear their sense in a particular way. If you read the poem out loud, your voice rises and falls not where you like but as the lineation demands.

What's more, the power of the lineation increases as the stanza moves forward, making the shape of the stanza feel not like a cookie cutter but like a dramatic linear process. Because the first and third lines of each stanza don't rhyme, we might not immediately notice that the second and fourth lines do, especially since the fifth line doesn't rhyme either.

> Eternity resembles
> One long Sunday afternoon.
> No traffic passes; the cigar smoke

> Curls in a blue cocoon.
> Children, have you nothing

But beginning with the sixth line, the rhymes move closer together, increasing the tension between syntax and line, binding the lines together more tightly at the same time that the length of the lines begins to vary.

> For our cold sakes?
> No tea? No little tea cakes?
> Sometimes now the rains disturb
> Even our remote suburb.

These two rhymed couplets in a row prepare our ears for the slam-dunk rhyme that shifts the way we apprehend the stanza's final sentence—

> There's a dampness underground.
> *The dead don't get around*
> *Much anymore.*

—but what matters here is not the simple fact that the third stanza ends with a trimeter followed by a dimeter line ("The dead don't get around / much anymore"), the second stanza with a dimeter followed a trimeter ("The dead don't get / Around much anymore"), and the first stanza with a monometer or single-stress line followed by a tetrameter ("The dead / Don't get around much anymore"). What matters is that the same sentence is made not only to sound slightly different in each case but to mean something slightly different in each case. The sound of the poem is its poignancy.

A poem like "Nostalgia and Complaint of the Grandparents" gets called traditional because it generally employs the whole poetic tool kit: rhyme, meter, and line (as well as lots of other tools). But the best poets who fought for the legitimacy of free verse in the early years of the twentieth century were not trying to make us choose between apparently different kinds of poetry; they were attempting to open our ears to a wider range of poetic possibilities. Following them, a poet like Justice learned as much from Williams and Pound as he did from Shakespeare and Keats, and one of the most important lessons was that the language of a particular poem may or may not demand the whole tool kit. If rhyme is jettisoned from a poem, what tactic must flex its muscles in order to keep the poetic contraption in the air? Meter. And if meter is foresworn? Line. And if line is abandoned? Syntax. And if syntax is abandoned? Diction. Sometimes it will be necessary for a poet to remember every tool in the kit; at other times it will be equally crucial to forget them, though nothing can be forgotten if it has not first been remembered.

Listen to seven sentences from Richard Howard's

"November, 1889," a dramatic monologue spoken by
the Victorian poet Robert Browning. The twenty-two
lines into which the sentences are divided do not follow a metrical pattern, and neither are they rhymed.

> Curious symptoms withal
> for migraine: patterns moving
> over surfaces, faint
> most often, fine designs
> that would come as a kind of cobweb
> cast iridescent upon the others, a net
> intervening between me and them.
> Lord! the things one sees when a fever-lit mind
> grants no middle distance.
> Prolixity of the real!
> And just when we are grateful
> for the dark, when night resumes us,
> comes prolixity
> of what is unreal,
> the melting waxworks of our sleep
> called dreams. I am against dreams,
> not being one to trust
> memory to itself.
> In my delirium, then, I had
> conviction of divided identity,
> never ceasing to be two persons who
> ever thwarted and opposed one another.

In these lines, Howard's Browning describes the world as it appears through sickness, but he also describes the poem in which he speaks: the poem is a net, a design, a moving pattern through which the world is perceived. And if Browning initially thinks that the mind might be cured, he eventually sees that anything we know—the past, each other, ourselves—we apprehend through "a net that covers the world." How is the "net" of this poem organized?

While the lines of "November, 1889" are not metered, the turns of the poem's syntax are draped across an intricate syllabic pattern. That is, the length of the line is determined not by counting stressed syllables but by counting syllables alone, no matter if they are stressed or unstressed; the syllables within the lines may, as in free verse, have any particular pattern of stress. Howard has not divided the poem into stanzas, but a repeated pattern of fourteen syllabic lines is the building block of the poem: a pair of seven-syllable lines is followed by a pair of six-syllable lines, then a quatrain of alternating nine- and eleven-syllable lines—

You can count the rest yourself. What matters here is not the syllable count as such but, once again, the tension between the syntax and the line endings determined by the count. That tension is the reason for this pattern of lines, and the aural pleasure we take in the poem is due to the way lines marshal the language into patterns of assonance and alliteration ("cast iridescent upon the others, a net") that don't necessarily have anything to do with the already given parameters of syntax. Line in relation to syntax, not syntax alone, is grouping the syllables in particular ways so that we hear those patterns. On the rare occasions when syllable count and syntax match ("Prolixity of the real!"), we feel the thrilling absence of the endless spill of enjambment that otherwise thrills us because of the way it determines intonation and stress. Were the line merely "cast iridescent upon others," there would be no tension, no rising of the voice toward the terminal syllable "net," which pushes us forward to the next line but also tugs us back to the sound of "cast" and "-scent."

I've said that "November, 1889" does not rhyme, at least in the conventional way—rhyming words placed at the ends of the lines. But there is enough sonic echo in the poem to make us mark the final syllables of certain lines with particular emphasis. I've also said that the poem is not metered, but it's important to note that a syntactically complete line in this poem ("Prolixity of the real!") feels like a resting point, just as a syntactically complete line does both in Shakespeare's metered verse ("When I do stare, see how the subject quakes!") and in Williams's free verse ("They taste good to her"). These three ways of thinking about the line in itself— metered verse, syllabic verse, free verse—have different effects, but in any case the line exists not because it has a certain pattern of stresses, a certain number of syllables, or an irregular number of stresses and syllables: the line exists because it has a relationship to syntax. You might say that a one-line poem doesn't really have anything we can discuss as a line, except inasmuch as we feel its relationship to lines in other poems. We need at least two lines to begin to hear how the line is functioning.

Lines can be short, as in Robert Herrick's "Upon His Departure Hence."

Thus I
Passe by
And die:
As One,
Unknown,
And gon:
I'm made
A shade,
And laid
I' th grave,
There have
My Cave.
Where tell
I dwell,
Farewell.

Lines can be long, as in this passage from William Blake's "The Book of Thel."

> Why a Tongue impress'd with honey from every wind?
> Why an Ear, a whirlpool fierce to draw creations in?
> Why a Nostril wide inhaling terror, trembling, &
>   affright?
> Why a tender curb upon the youthful burning boy?
> Why a little curtain of flesh on the bed of our desire?

And lines can be even longer than that, as in this passage from Allen Ginsberg's "Sunflower Sutra."

> I walked the banks of the tincan banana dock and sat
>   down under the huge shade of a Southern Pacific
>   locomotive to look at the sunset over the box
>   house hills and cry.
> Jack Kerouac sat beside me on a busted rusty iron
>   pole, companion, we thought the same thoughts
>   of the soul, bleak and blue and sad-eyed,
>   surrounded by the gnarled steel roots of trees
>   of machinery.
> The oily water on the river mirrored the red sky, sun
>   sank on top of final Frisco peaks, no fish in that
>   stream, no hermit in those mounts, just ourselves
>   rheumy-eyed and hungover like old bums on the
>   riverbank, tired and wily.

> Look at the Sunflower, he said, there was a dead gray
> > shadow against the sky, big as a man, sitting dry
> > on top of a pile of ancient sawdust—
> —I rushed up enchanted—it was my first sunflower,
> > memories of Blake—my visions—Harlem
> and Hells of the Eastern rivers, bridges clanking Joes
> > Greasy Sandwiches, dead baby carriages, blank
> > treadles tires forgotten and unretreaded, the
> > poem of the riverbank, condoms & pots, steel
> > knives, nothing stainless, only the dank muck and
> > the razor-sharp artifacts passing into the past . . .

The danger with Herrick's monometer (or single-stress) lines, grouped in rhymed triplets, is that the line endings manipulate the syntax with such rapidity that the poem seems tricky. And the danger with Blake's fourteeners (or seven-stress lines) is that the line may too easily break in two, making the lines sound like the more familiar ballad meter: alternating four- and three-stress lines. And the danger with Ginsberg's attenuated free-verse lines is that they might stop functioning as lines, maintaining no particular relationship to the syntax. But Herrick's quietly natural syntax keeps his poem from feeling merely like a feat. And Blake's repositioning of the caesura (or pause) within each line prevents his fourteeners from breaking into regular pieces, while his repetition of a syntactical pattern plays against the irregularity. And the first three lines of Ginsberg's poem, all of them syntactically complete, establish a stable relationship between line and syntax—a launching pad for the ecstatic fourth sentence, enjambed across several lines. The length of the line does not in itself have a predictable effect.

Nor does the variation of the length of the line within a single poem, as in this rhymed and metered stanza from George Herbert's "The Collar."

> I struck the board, and cry'd, No more.
> I will abroad.
> What? shall I ever sigh and pine?
> My lines and life are free; free as the rode,
> Loose as the winde, as large as store.

Or in this rhymed and syllabic stanza from Marianne Moore's "The Past is the Present."

> If external action is effete
> and rhyme is outmoded,
> I shall revert to you,
> Habakkuk, as on a recent occasion I was goaded
> into doing, by XY, who was speaking of
> unrhymed verse.

Or in this free-verse passage from George Oppen's "Of Being Numerous."

> Yet I am one of those who from nothing but man's
>   way of thought and one of his dialects and what
>   has happened to me
> Have made poetry
>
> To dream of that beach
> For the sake of an instant in the eyes,
>
> The absolute singular
>
> The unearthly bonds
> Of the singular
>
> Which is the bright light of shipwreck

In each of these passages the lines feel inevitable, not because the author has made a decision to use a long line or a short line or a mixture of long and short lines: the length of the line establishes a relationship to the syntax, and that relationship is guided by the author's sense of how the syntax should be paced—how the given syllables of the words should be organized so that we hear the pattern of their stresses in one way rather than another way.

Oppen begins with a line that, like Ginsberg's line in "Sunflower Sutra," is so very long that it threatens to flatten out into prose, the relationships between its stressed syllables all but lost in a welter of unstressed syllables.

> Yet I am one of those who from nothing but man's
> way of thought and one of his dialects and what
> has happened to me

But by following this line with a line almost as short as Herrick's, a line whose brevity is emphasized by the unexpected rhyme between the final syllable of its final word ("poetry") and the final syllable of the long line preceding it ("me")—

> Have made poetry

—Oppen suddenly tightens the rhythmic texture of the poem. This line feels epigrammatic not only because of what it says but because we now hear stressed syllables in close proximity to one another: "Have MADE POetry." As a result, these lines seem to enact what the sentence is about: the lines make poetry, moving from a tenuous concatenation of ingredients to a terse declaration of purpose.

The subsequent lines of the passage enact a similar movement between constriction and release. Following a group of short enjambed lines that in this case embody the hesitancy of the process of thought—

> The absolute singular

> The unearthly bonds
> Of the singular

—the final line sounds like a resting place because its greater length allows for syntactical completion and a more resonant pattern of stressed syllables.

> Which is the BRIGHT LIGHT of SHIPwreck

The two stresses in the middle of the line are not only wedged against each other without any intervening unstressed syllables, they also rhyme with each other: "bright light." Then the vowel in the final stress of the line ("ship") pulls our ears back to the vowel sound in the first two syllables of the line ("which is"). In contrast to the lines preceding it, this line feels balanced, a completed pattern of sound. So while the opening lines of this passage feel satisfying because of the movement from a very long line to a very short line, the final lines feel satisfying because of the movement from a sequence of short lines to a longer line.

Though we may not notice it at first, rhyme plays

just as important a role in Oppen's lines as it does in Herbert's metered lines or Moore's syllabic lines. And though the length of Oppen's lines is not determined by the counting of stresses or syllables, there is nothing casual about the number of stresses and syllables in each of his lines. Deciding where the line should end in a free-verse poem might initially seem more mysterious than in a metered or syllabic poem, but in fact it is not: whether or not the line ending is determined by an arbitrary constraint, the line ending won't have a powerful function unless we hear it playing off the syntax in relationship to other line endings.

Reconsider the end of King Lear's speech.

Beneath is all the fiend's.
There's hell, there's darkness, there is the sulphurous pit.
Burning, scalding, stench, consumption—
Fie, fie, fie; pah, pah!
Give me an ounce of civet, good
Apothecary, sweeten my imagination.

Here, I've lineated the sentences that are sometimes printed as Shakespeare's prose, but instead of organizing the language in iambic pentameter lines, I've made lines that encourage us to hear variations from that pattern of stressed and unstressed syllables. To hear the first line as a pentameter—

> Beneath is all the fiend's. There's hell, there's darkness

—is to hear the syntax rise to the final word of the line ("darkness") and fall away onto the next phrase: "There is the sulphurous pit." In contrast, to hear the first line as a syntactically complete declaration followed by a triplet of parallel phrases in the second line—

> Beneath is all the fiend's.
> There's hell, there's darkness, there is the sulphurous pit.

—is to hear the syntax rise from "hell" to "darkness" to "pit" in a line that is not only syntactically complete but also more syntactically complex. As my version continues, the next line moves from three parts (hell, darkness, pit) to four—

> Burning, scalding, stench, consumption—

—and I've taken the liberty of concluding this line with a dash that pushes us forward to the fifth line's five monosyllabic words: "fie, fie, fie; pah, pah!" Then, in the final two lines, I've introduced the first and only enjambment in a passage in which syntax and line have been equivalent.

> Give me an ounce of civet, good
> Apothecary, sweeten my imagination.

Enjambment is not in itself valuable: like everything else in a poem, its power depends on its relationship to other formal aspects of the poem—more specifically, the nature of the line endings surrounding it. I might have chosen to lineate the final sentence this way.

> Give me an ounce of civet, good apothecary,
> Sweeten my imagination.

Or this way.

> Give me an ounce of civet,
> Good apothecary, sweeten my imagination.

But by introducing the strong enjambment—

> Give me an ounce of civet, good
> Apothecary, sweeten my imagination.

—I've broken the pattern established by the earlier lineation and introduced a moment of formal tension as the passage concludes. The syntax of the penultimate line feels balanced, since its final word alliterates strongly with its initial word ("Give me an ounce of civet, good"); at the same time the syntax feels broken, the line ending pushing us to the concluding line with a force that has not hitherto been utilized in the passage. Because the line ends on the adjective "good," we tend to put more stress on that syllable than we would if it were followed in the line by the noun it modifies: "apothecary."

GIVE me an OUNCE of CIVet, GOOD

As a result, we hear the alliteration of "good" with "give" more powerfully, just as we hear the rhyme between the two other stressed syllables in the line ("give" and "civ"). Our ears are pulled back to the beginning of the line by similar sounds, and at the same time they are pushed forward to the next line by the strong enjambment. Sonic echo is working with line in order to determine the particular way we hear the syntax.

There is not necessarily one way to do this.

Give me an ounce of civet, good apothecary, sweeten
My imagination.

This arrangement sacrifices what to my ear is the more attractively complex music of a line whose syntax feels both balanced and broken; but this attenuation of the penultimate line, ending with an even more dramatic enjambment on the verb ("sweeten"), is worth considering. In fact, I wouldn't have settled on my preferred arrangement without considering it. The weighing of such alternatives goes on in the composition of any line, whether or not its length is determined by a metrical or syllabic pattern. Robert Frost once said rather impishly that writing free verse is like playing tennis with the net down; in fact, writing any kind of poem is more like playing tennis on a court in which the net is in motion at the same time that the ball is in motion.

Listen finally to the opening lines of "Nostos," a free-verse poem by Louise Glück. The title is the Greek word for homecoming.

> There was an apple tree in the yard—
> this would have been
> forty years ago—behind,
> only meadow. Drifts
> of crocus in the damp grass.
> I stood at the window:
> late April. Spring
> flowers in the neighbor's yard.
> How many times, really, did the tree
> flower on my birthday,
> the exact day, not
> before, not after? Substitution
> of the immutable
> for the shifting, the evolving.
> Substitution of the image
> For relentless earth. What
> do I know of this place,

the role of the tree for decades
taken by a bonsai, voices
rising from the tennis courts—
Fields. Smell of the tall grass, new cut.

This passage is made of twenty-one lines. It is also made of nine sentences, some of which are syntactically incomplete, the first of which is a run-on sentence. As in the pentameter version of the passage from *King Lear*, there is no regular relationship between the sentences and the lines. The sentences do not exceed or fall short of the lines in a predictable way, and neither is the way in which the lines end predictable: some end with a full stop, others with a comma or a dash, and still others with no punctuation at all. But like King Lear's speech, Glück's poem begins with a syntactically complete line. It proposes the presence in the past of something that no longer exists in the present, and it could not do so in more plainly.

There was an apple tree in the yard

Following this moment of sonic stability, however, the poem not only describes a more tenuous process of thought, it also makes us hear the shifting hesitancy of the process in lines that disrupt our natural apprehension of the syntax.

> Substitution
> of the immutable
> for the shifting, the evolving.
> Substitution of the image
> for relentless earth.

So while we hear the sound of certainty at the beginning of the poem ("There was an apple tree"), we feel here the evolving drama of discovery as that certainty unravels. Unlike Shakespeare, Glück is dramatizing the encroachment not of madness but of self-doubt, and in both cases the lineation is determining the pulse of thought, the interplay of different kinds of line endings creating different ways of apprehending syntax as thinking. Not this—

> What do I know of this place,
> The role of the tree for decades taken by a bonsai,
> Voices rising from the tennis courts

—but this: lines that become a runway for the sonic boom of revelation with which the poem concludes.

> What
> do I know of this place,
> the role of the tree for decades
> taken by a bonsai, voices

> rising from the tennis courts—
> Fields. Smell of the tall grass, new cut.
> As one expects of a lyric poet.
> We look at the world once, in childhood.
> The rest is memory.

Here, at the end of "Nostos," we return to syntactically complete lines: the opening line makes an observation about the past, and the three concluding lines offer a sequence of declarations about the mental processes through which we come to understand the relationship between the past and the present. In between, the enjambed sentences embody that wayward process.

As is the case in Lear's speech, however, these concluding lines have a different effect from the syntactically complete line with which the poem opens. At the beginning of "Nostos," the confluence of syntax and line suggests a security about knowledge and memory that the poem persists to unravel; in retrospect, that security sounds unexamined, the plain declaration of existence weirdly naïve: "There was an apple tree." At the end of the poem, in contrast, the confluence of syntax and line sounds rueful, the hard-won product of thought rather than a declaration masking the necessity of more thinking: "As one expects of a lyric poet." It's not that the poem has concluded by saying anything particularly challenging: one has only to imagine a poem beginning with the line "We look at the world once, in childhood" to feel that the poem is thrilling because of the way it moves to its concluding wisdom, not because of the wisdom as such. The line is no arbitrary unit, no ruler, but a dynamic force that works in conjunction with other elements of the poem: the syntax of the sentences, the rhythm of stressed and unstressed syllables, and the resonance of similar sounds.

So far, I've spoken of lines as enjambed and end-stopped, but because the line's effect depends on the variable qualities of the poem's other elements, there may be different kinds of enjambment, different ways in which the syntax breaks across the end of the line. There are also different ways in which a line might be end-stopped. Finally, there are as many discriminations to be made as there are lines in poems. The next chapter will propose a few broad categories.

Ending the Line

"At a particular time, at a particular date, in a particular room," remembered Ezra Pound, "two authors, neither engaged in picking the other's pocket, decided that the dilution of *vers libre* . . . had gone too far and that some counter-current must be set going." The time was around 1917; the two authors, Ezra Pound and T. S. Eliot. To them, modernist free verse had already entered its decadence. It was being written thoughtlessly, flaccidly, and the counter-current was soon to appear in Pound's *Hugh Selwyn Mauberley* and Eliot's little book called simply *Poems:* rhymed quatrains.

Listen to a passage from Pound's *Mauberley.*

Thick foliage
Placid beneath warm suns,
Tawn fore-shores
Washed in the cobalt of oblivions;

Or through dawn-mist
The grey and rose
Of the juridical
Flamingoes;

A consciousness disjunct,
Being but this overblotted
Series
Of intermittences;

Coracle of Pacific voyages,
The unforecasted beach;
Then on an oar
Read this:

"I was
And I no more exist;
Here drifted
An hedonist."

Pound's quatrains are generally rhymed X A X A (the second and fourth lines rhyming with each other while the first and third remain unrhymed), but the lines follow no regular meter: the regularly rhymed lines contain a fluctuating number of stresses—as few as one or as many as five. Nor do the lines ever scan in exactly the same way. The relationship of stressed to unstressed syllables also fluctuates, and even the lines that flirt with the rhythm of the pentameter—

CORacle OF paCIFic VOYagES

—don't have a metrical context in which they truly function as pentameter lines. The poem sets up an expectation for a repeated pattern and simultaneously disrupts that expectation, and we are consequently asked to hear more stresses in certain lines than are actually there. Listening to the final quatrain, for instance, we may expect three stresses in the final line ("An hedonist") so that it matches the three firm stresses in the second line, with which it rhymes so crisply.

And I no MORE exIST.

As a result, we put an unnaturally heavy stress on the first syllable of the final line ("an") and feel a gaping caesura or pause between this syllable and the next, which also needs to be stressed.

AN HEdonIST

The line floats away, drawn out in a languorous hesitancy much like the sensibility the poem describes.

It's sometimes said that a poet would be well served by mastering the techniques of meter and rhyme before tackling free verse, just as it's said that a painter ought to master representational techniques before delving into abstraction. But these lines from *Hugh*

Selwyn Mauberley demonstrate an equally plausible wisdom: the extraordinary rhythmic delicacy, which depends on the control of the line, could not have been achieved without an ongoing devotion to the craft of free verse. For at the same time that they turned to rhymed quatrains, Eliot and Pound also continued to write free verse: their countercurrent announced that the quality of a poem had nothing to do with the form it happened to take. Once revolutionary, free verse had quickly become an orthodoxy, a set of formal procedures that might be employed as ineptly or as brilliantly as rhymed quatrains. But this judgment rests on the wonder of achievement: in just a few years free verse had become as powerful an instrument as rhymed quatrains.

The achievement was bigger than Pound and Eliot sitting in a particular room in a particular time. Working beside them, Williams, Moore, and Stevens developed a variety of distinctive free-verse lines, each of which is determined by a particular manner of ending the line, each of which may produce different effects in relationship to different kinds of syntax or patterns of stress. The variety of effects is potentially infinite. Here, I will focus on the shifting effects of three ways of ending the line: annotating lines, parsing lines, and end-stopped lines. I will begin by describing poems that adhere fairly closely to one kind of line ending, but ultimately I want to show how the power of free verse most often depends on the interplay of these different kinds of line endings.

Consider first the kind of free-verse lines Pound was writing at around the same time that he wrote the quatrains of *Hugh Selwyn Mauberley.*

> And all that day
> Nicea moved before me
> And the cold grey air troubled her not
> For all her naked beauty, but not the tropic skin,
> And the long slender feet lit on the curb's marge
> And her moving height went before me,
>> We alone having being.
> And all that day, another day:
>> Thin husks I had known as men,
> Dry casques of departed locusts
>> speaking a shell of speech . . .
> Propped between chairs and tables . . .
> Words like the locust-shells, moved by no inner being;
>> A dryness calling for death.

While the lines of *Mauberley* tend to be short and heavily enjambed, Pound's characteristic free-verse line tends like Whitman's to be syntactically complete. A strong punctuation mark almost always occurs at the end of the line, and on the few occasions when it doesn't, the line ending makes more emphatic the normative turn of syntax: "departed locusts / speaking a shell of speech." Having drastically reduced the tension between syntax and line, Pound inevitably tends toward a longer line, a line built from a variety of smaller units of syntax, a line that privileges its self-contained rhythmic pattern over the poem's forward momentum. Almost every line I've quoted from Canto VII scans differently from the one before it, but all the lines sound exactly like Pound.

Listen in contrast to the characteristic free-verse line of Williams's *Spring and All*.

> The sunlight in a
> yellow plaque upon the
> varnished floor
>
> is full of a song
> inflated to
> fifty pounds pressure
>
> at the faucet of
> June that rings
> the triangle of the air
>
> pulling at the
> anemones in
> Persephone's cow pasture—

When from among
The steel rocks leaps
J. P. M.

who enjoyed
extraordinary privileges
among virginity

to solve the core
of whirling flywheels
by cutting

the Gordian knot
with a Veronese or
perhaps a Rubens—

Williams bends his syntax relentlessly across the line, and the line endings generally do not perform the work of punctuation or emphasize the turns of normative syntax. While the rhythmic vitality of Pound's line is due to the variety of syntactical patterns within it, Williams uses enjambment to determine the placement of rhythmic stress, playing the irregularity of his line endings against the chaste decorum of his three-line stanzas. Having capitalized on the tension between syntax and line, Williams inevitably tends toward a shorter line, one narrow enough to exclude almost any suggestion of syntactical pattern ("varnished floor"; "the Gordian knot"; "J. P. M.").

Sometimes the enjambment throws emphasis on the beginning of the line: here, the first two lines end with unstressed syllables, and the line endings encourage us to give additional emphasis to the stressed syllable with which the second and third lines begins ("YELlow"; "VARnished").

> The sunlight in a
> yellow plaque upon the
> varnished floor

At other times, Williams throws emphasis on the end of the line by concluding with a heavily stressed syllable and beginning the next line with an unstressed syllable ("SONG / in").

> is full of a song
> inflated to

By holding us back, these lines keep us racing forward. And if the static quality of Pound's end-stopped line feels appropriate to his characteristic subject (the return of ancient spiritual presences to a timeless present), Williams's rush of blunt enjambments feels crucial to his: the threat of J. Pierpont Morgan's antiquarian taste to the energy of contemporary art.

Williams's enjambments follow one another with a rapidity that may feel overwhelming, but the nature of many of his line endings is not different from one variety of Milton's. For Satan, Milton explains in *Paradise Lost*, conscience

> wakes the bitter memory
> Of what he was, what is, and what must be

—or so we might reason, stopping at what appears to be a concluding point of syntax at the end of the pentameter line; but the syntax continues.

> Of what he was, what is, and what must be
> Worse.

This enjambment provides both the stillness of a completed clause and the thrill of discovering that the syntax continues. The lines sound like a discovery because the second line begins with a heavily stressed syllable— a stress that takes us by surprise, since we expect an unstressed syllable at the beginning of this iambic pentameter line.

John Hollander has said that Milton's enjambments "annotate" his syntax. That is, rather than following the grammatical units, the lines cut against them, annotating the syntax with emphasis that the syntax itself would not otherwise provide. The same thing may be

said of the lines in *Spring and All,* and the achievement
was not easily won. Consider one of the many poems
called "Pastoral" that Williams wrote in the earlier years
of his career: rather than cutting up the syntax into unexpected or fragmentary pieces, as the annotating lines
do in *Spring and All,* these lines generally contain coherent pieces of syntax.

> The old man who goes about
> Gathering dog lime
> Walks in the gutter
> Without looking up
> And his tread
> Is more majestic than
> That of the Episcopal minister
> Approaching the pulpit
> Of a Sunday.
> Meanwhile
> The little sparrows
> Hop ingenuously
> About the pavement
> Quarreling
> Over those things
> That interest them
> With sharp voices
> But we who are wiser
> Shut ourselves in
> On either hand

And no one knows
Whether we think good
Or evil.
                    These things
Astonish me beyond words!

J. V. Cunningham once said that lines like these "parse" the syntax of a poem. That is, while the lines are not end-stopped, they generally follow the normative turns of the syntax, breaking it at predictable points rather than cutting against it. While the more aggressive annotating line asks us to stress syllables we wouldn't ordinarily stress—

The sunlight in a
yellow plaque upon the
varnished floor

—the parsing line tends to emphasize the given contour of the sentence, reinforcing the way it would sound if it were written out as prose.

And no one knows
Whether we think good
Or evil.
                    These things
Astonish me beyond words!

Neither a parsing nor an annotating line is inevitably preferable; there is nothing wrong or right about any particular way of ending the line. But by placing line so utterly in service of syntax, reducing the tension between syntax and line, a poem dominated by the parsing line can make its own lineation seem increasingly unnecessary. Without the drama of discovery provided by more radically annotating lines, Williams must end the early "Pastoral" with an inflated sense of closure: "These things / Astonish me beyond words!" He has discovered here his characteristic subject matter and diction (both strategically plain), but he has not yet discovered a way to make the poem enact his feeling of astonishment.

The final lines of the poem from *Spring and All* make the same point as the final lines of "Pastoral" (little things may be as astonishing as a capitalist's acquisition of a Veronese), but the sentiment no longer feels contrived. It feels integral to the poem rather than layered onto it.

And so it comes
to motor cars—
which is the son

leaving off the g
of sunlight and grass—
Impossible

to say, impossible
to underestimate—
wind, earthquakes in

Manchuria, a
partridge
from dry leaves

Even as it concludes, this poem is all motion, a careening sequence of metaphors of things in motion, the confidant repetitions of "impossible" at the end of the line giving way to line endings that annotate the syntax in increasingly edgy ways: "earthquakes in / Manchura, a / partridge." The excessive use of the annotating line can come to seem mannered or fussy, a way of jazzing up uninteresting syntax, just as the excessive use of the parsing line can come to feel dull, a way of merely repeating what the syntax is already doing on its own. But in these lines from *Spring and All,* Williams's playfulness is functional. His aggressively annotating lineation—the division of articles from nouns, syllables from words, letters from syllables—drives not only the movement but the content of the poem: the "sunlight" is full of "song" and Morgan's motorcars are the "son / leaving off the g" of the word "song" (or "son / g"), which is "sunlight." Williams suggests by the free association of syllables that industrial culture may be astonishing after all.

These annotating lines could not be more different from Pound's end-stopped lines or Williams's earlier parsing lines. What changed Williams's prosody so radically in such a short time? What allowed him to distinguish syntax from line independent of grammatical units? Listen to the opening stanzas of Marianne Moore's "The Fish."

The Fish

wade
through black jade.
    Of the crow blue mussel shells, one
        keeps
        adjusting the ash heaps;
    opening and shutting itself like

an
injured fan.
    The barnacles which encrust the
        side
        of the wave cannot hide
    there; for the submerged shafts of the

sun,
split like spun
    glass, move themselves with spotlight swift-
        ness

> into the crevices—
> in and out, illuminating
>
> the
> turquoise sea
>   of bodies. The water drives a
>   wedge
>   of iron through the iron edge
>   of the cliff, whereupon the stars,
>
> pink
> rice grains, ink
>   bespattered jelly-fish, crabs like
>   green
>   lilies and submarine
>   toadstools, slide each on the other.

Like the lines I examined from Richard Howard's "November, 1886," these lines are organized syllabically: the
six lines of each stanza contain (in order) one, three,
eight, one, six, and eight syllables. Only a handful of the
lines are end-stopped, and few of them could be said to
be parsing the poem's syntax. Instead, the lines range
from the kind of enjambment Milton employed—

> of the wave cannot hide
> there

—to the more aggressively annotating line that Williams began to favor in *Spring and All,* partly because of Moore's example.

> The barnacles which encrust the
> side

In addition, the poem is also rhymed (A A X B B X), making the ends of these annotating lines even more palpably audible and consequently forcing us to place strong accents on syllables that we would otherwise be at liberty to neglect. The effect of the lineation of the first two lines—

> wade
> through black jade

—is familiar from the irregularly metered and rhymed lines of Robert Frost's "After Apple Picking," where meter and rhyme conspire to mark the end of the line more insistently.

> Cherish in hand, lift down, and not let fall.
> For all
> That struck the earth

But the effect of "an / injured fan" or "ness / into the crevices" pushes a familiar principle to an extreme, highlighting unexpected syllables and slowing down the poem's momentum. "Marianne's words remain separate," said Williams in one of the prose sections of *Spring and All*, "each unwilling to group with the others except as they move in the one direction."

At times, Moore's and Williams's lines annotate the syntax so radically, dividing words into syllables, that the line endings can threaten to seem arbitrary rather than functional. But unlike Frost, Moore and Williams sometimes want their formal gestures to feel more calculated than organic: rather than allowing us to take the formal procedures of art for granted, they want us to feel the imposition of pattern on language, and that imposition forces us to ask questions we might profitably ask of any poem, no matter how natural or inevitable its procedures might seem. How can one tell when the effect created by the relationship between syntax and line is driven by necessity? How can one make arbitrariness itself a necessity?

Consider the opening five-line stanzas of Moore's "When I Buy Pictures."

When I Buy Pictures

or what is closer to the truth, when I look at
   that of which I may regard myself as the
      imaginary possessor, I fix upon that which
         would

give me pleasure in my average moments: the
satire upon curiosity,
in which no more is discernible than the
intensity of the mood;

or quite the opposite—the old thing, the mediaeval decorated hat box, in which there
are hounds with waists diminishing like the
waist of the hour-glass
and deer, both white and brown, and birds and
seated people; it may be no more than a
square
of parquetry; the literal biography perhaps—
in letters stand-

ing well apart upon a parchment-like expanse;
or that which is better without words, which means
just as much or just as little as it is understood to
mean by the observer—the grave of Adam,
prefigured by himself; a bed of beans
or artichokes in six varieties of blue; the snipe-
legged hiero-

glyphic in three parts; it may be anything.

In contrast to the syllabic design of "The Fish," the syllabic design of "When I Buy Pictures" produces a stanza

made of extremely long lines: the syllable counts of the
lines in each stanza are twelve, eleven, fifteen, twenty-
one, and eighteen. Since the line endings consequently
occur much less frequently throughout the ongoing
movement of the syntax, it's harder to hear what the
endings are doing to the syntax, and, as a result, the
lines feel more arbitrary, an imposition on the poem's
syntax rather than a strategic alteration of its movement. Similarly, although the poem is rhymed, it's almost impossible to hear the rhymes: the fact that the
opening stanza rhymes "the" (or "thee") with "curiosity" is undetectable unless we notice the slightly stron-
ger rhymes placed in the same positions in subsequent
stanzas (in which "there" rhymes more obviously with
"square" and "means" with "beans"). It's consequently
hard to say that the line endings in "When I Buy Pictures"
annotate the syntax because their effect seems willfully
arbitrary.

Or should I say delightfully arbitrary? In itself, the
arbitrary is not a problem: there must be room for
such effects in poetry. But even the arbitrary must be
driven by necessity, and necessity can be judged only
on a poem by poem basis: what does the language of
this particular poem require at this particular junc-
ture? Moore asked this question of herself, for when
she reprinted "When I Buy Pictures," she discarded
its syllabic design, buried its rhymes, and recast the

poem in an end-stopped line that is distinctively her own—a line that sounds nothing like Pound's end-stopped line.

When I Buy Pictures

or what is closer to the truth,
when I look at that which I may regard myself as the
     imaginary possessor,
I fix upon what would give me pleasure in my average
     moments:
the satire upon curiosity, in which no more is
     discernible than the intensity of the mood;
or quite the opposite—the old thing, the mediaeval
     decorated hat-box,
in which there are hounds with waists diminishing
     like the waist of the hour-glass
and deer and birds and seated people;
it may be no more than a square of parquetry; the
     literal biography perhaps—
in letters standing well apart upon a parchment-like
     expanse;
an artichoke in six varieties of blue; the snipe-legged
     hieroglyphic in three parts;
the silver fence protecting Adam's grave or Michael
     taking Adam by the wrist.

Too stern an intellectual emphasis upon this quality
    or that, detracts from one's enjoyment;
it must not wish to disarm anything; nor may the
    approved triumph easily be honoured—
that which is great because something else is small.

Moore herself never explained why she turned from syllabic verse to this end-stopped free verse, but her poems themselves provide some clues. Consider the first line of "When I Buy Pictures," which continues from the title and begins with the word "or": "or what is closer to the truth, / when I look at that which I may regard myself as the imaginary possessor." This poem is highly ambivalent about the act of ownership, and I suspect that in this particular case the poem's syllabic design seemed to enact a kind of aesthetic possession that the poem itself has taken pains to reject. Moore disapproves of anything "which is great because something else is small," and the syllabic organization was itself in danger of seeming like a feat. In contrast, these end-stopped lines have the advantage of organizing Moore's long catalogue of beloved objects more plainly, less aggressively. As a result, our attention is thrown where the poem's argument suggests that Moore would want it thrown: away from the maker to the things that are made. The formal mechanism of the poem feels more organically related to the material, less brilliantly calculated.

But are highly discursive free-verse lines really any less of a feat than syllabic lines? Are the lines from *Hugh Selwyn Mauberley* any more or less sophisticated than the lines from Canto VII? Can any good poem avoid the impression that its maker has organized its language in intricate ways, even if the maker's goal has been to disguise the imposition of pattern, making it seem natural? Every poet is caught in this dilemma, and gratefully so. Like the seventeenth-century poet George Herbert, who wrote fancy poems about wanting to speak plainly, Moore made poems that enact this paradox in their formal decisions. It's hard to know which version of "When I Buy Pictures" one should prefer. Moore herself went on to write great poems in free verse, and she also went on to write great poems in syllabics. She may have felt that the plain coincidence of syntax and line improved "When I Buy Pictures," but she was unwilling to make categorical aesthetic decisions, as if to say that one kind of line was inevitably superior to another kind of line. Her end-stopped line had one effect, and her annotating line had another.

Today, this freedom to choose from among a wide range of formal possibilities rather than between them is crucial. Even a century ago, when Pound and Eliot decided that the dilution of free verse had already gone too far, they would have witnessed the maturity of several distinct species of line: Pound's end-stopped line, Moore's end-stopped line, Williams's annotating line, and the parsing line of Williams's earlier poems. In addition, Eliot had developed a distinctive free-verse line from the post-Shakespearean blank verse of John Webster, a line that invokes a regular meter in order to avoid it. With such a sophisticated and varied free-verse vocabulary in place, what were Pound and Eliot complaining about when they returned to the writing of rhymed quatrains?

In part, their countercurrent was designed to remind writers of free verse that the embrace of innovation did not inevitably entail a rejection of the pleasures of metrical writing. In addition, they were pointing out the danger of relying too exclusively or programmatically on any one kind line ending. The only poem I've examined that might have raised their hackles is Williams's early "Pastoral"—not because it uses a parsing line, but because it parses its syntax so consistently that the poem cannot generate the energy required to make its subject matter seem worthy of its own notice. Wallace Stevens and H. D. (as well as a host of lesser poets) also used a parsing line more often than not, and in itself the line is not to be scorned: by serving up a poem's syntax in clearly apprehendable units, the parsing line may allow us to inhabit a syntactically complex argument more viscerally.

But whatever its strengths, no particular kind of line needs to be championed at the expense of other kinds. While I have for strategic purposes examined poems that highlight different kinds of lines egregiously (end-stopped, parsing, annotating), my point is that poems need not confine themselves to any one of these procedures. Finally, no particular line is valuable except inasmuch as it performs a dramatic function in relationship to other lines in a particular poem: one kind of line ending becomes powerful because of its relationship to other kinds of line endings.

We have seen this to be the case in Shakespeare: the speech from *King Lear* moves (we can now say) from end-stopped lines through parsing and annotating lines, gradually increasing the tension between syntax and line as it moves forward. We've seen that the same kind of movement distinguishes Glück's "Nostos."

> Substitution
> of the immutable
> for the shifting, the evolving.
> Substitution of the image
> For relentless earth. What
> do I know of this place,

the role of the tree for decades
taken by a bonsai, voices
rising from the tennis courts—
Fields. Smell of the tall grass, new cut.
As one expects of a lyric poet.
We look at the world once, in childhood.
The rest is memory.

Glück's poem ends with a line of concluding wisdom that in itself might resemble the concluding gesture of Williams's "Pastoral": the crucial difference is that her poem moves from line endings that parse the syntax—

Substitution
of the immutable

—to line endings that annotate the syntax—

What
do I know

—before settling back into the end-stopped line with which the poem also began.

We look at the world once, in childhood.

The poem is not written out of a categorical decision to use one kind of line rather than another, and, as a result, the poem's concluding wisdom does not feel layered over the poem's content. Instead, it feels like a statement that the reader of the poem has, like the author, worked to achieve. This work is the pleasure of poetry, and the end of the line is where the work of pleasure takes place.

As "Nostos" demonstrates, the purpose—the thrill— of a free verse prosody lies in the ability to shape the movement of a poem through the strategic use of different kinds of line endings. The line's control of intonation creates the expectation for meaningfulness, allowing a poem's language to wander from its more workaday organizational tasks. And when the different kinds of line endings I've examined are used in consort with one another, then all line endings become a means of annotating syntax. That is, in the context of lines that cut up the syntax in provocative ways, a simple parsing line that does nothing to syntax may be the most attention-grabbing line of all—just as an annotating line is more obviously provocative in the context of a lot of end-stopped lines. The drama of lineation lies in the simultaneous making and breaking of our expectation for pattern.

Consider the practice of Frank Bidart. Typed out as prose, Bidart's syntax is often difficult to follow, but set in lines, it becomes a pattern of sound that organizes our experience of the poem before we have time to worry about the subject matter. Near the end of Bidart's long poem "Confessional," for instance, comes a fifty-seven-line sentence based on a famous prose sentence from the ninth chapter of St. Augustine's *Confessions.* The sentence is complex enough in the original Latin—a periodic sentence that interposes six dependent clauses before introducing the main subject and verb. Replicating this structure, Bidart fleshes out the dependent clauses, making them longer and more syntactically complex than in the original version. The six dependent clauses, each beginning with the word "if," range from two to seventeen lines, but the independent clause (the main subject and verb) appears on a single line. If "this" that we hear is the voice of God, proclaim the first fifty-six lines of the sentence in so many more words, then

> would not *this* be: *ENTER THOU INTO THE JOY OF THY LORD?*

This final line appears as a tremendous relief, but it also makes us crave the tension built up in the preceding fifty-six lines of the sentence. For while that tension is proliferated by the succession of dependent clauses, it is at the same time tightly controlled by Bidart's strategic lineation of the syntax within those clauses. In addition, like Emily Dickinson before him, Bidart employs idiosyncratic punctuation and capitalization in order to control further our experience of the poem's syntax. As a result, we feel that the wisdom of the sentence lies not precisely in what it says but in the endlessly reticulated process of arriving at what it says.

That process consists of an intricate dance of pattern and variation, the lineation of each clause both building on and departing from the clause preceding it. The first dependent clause is also the briefest: two lines parse the clause.

> If any man could shut his ears
>
> to the tumult of the flesh—;

The second dependent clause is eleven lines long, and it begins by parsing the syntax in the same way, ending the first line before the beginning of a prepositional phrase ("to the tumult"; "of earth and sea").

> if suddenly the cacophony
>
> of earth and sea and air
>
> were SILENT, and the voice of the self
> died to the self, and so the self

found its way beyond the self,—

beyond the SELF it has made,—

SILENT

our expiations and confessions,
the voice that says: *NO REMISSION OF SINS*
WITHOUT THE SHEDDING OF BLOOD,

the WORD that was only given us drenched in blood,—

After the initial parsing lines, these lines begin annotating the syntax more boldly, breaking apart subjects and
verbs ("the self / died"; "the self // found") and increasing the tension by reinforcing the second annotating
line with a stanza division. Then, after the syntax is in-
terrupted by an apposition set as its own line ("beyond
the SELF it has made"), we meet the most aggressively
annotating line in the clause, its single word thrown
into uppercase for additional emphasis: "SILENT / our
expiations and confessions." Finally, the clause settles
back down into parsing and end-stopped lines, preparing us for what we might on first reading expect to be
the subject of the independent clause.

Instead, we begin a third dependent clause, and each
of the subsequent clauses offers a similar sequence of line
endings, providing a pattern for the mounting tension

caused by the continued delay of the subject: parsing lines are followed by annotating lines that finally give way to end-stopped lines. This pattern allows us to experience the mounting tension not as disorder but as a reliable sequence of waves: while each dependent clause contributes to the overall tension of the periodic sentence, the lineation within each dependent clause strategically curbs and increases that tension in smaller increments. Interweaving three different kinds of line ending in what becomes a familiar pattern, Bidart orchestrates intonation, speed, and our expectation for syntactical repetition.

Listen to the way in which the last two dependent clauses spill into the concluding one-line independent clause. The first of these dependent clauses is seventeen lines long while the second is just five lines long.

. . . if in this SILENCE,

He whom we *crave* to hear

SPOKE AT LAST—;

spoke not through the VEIL
of earth and sea and air,

thunder, 'SIGNS AND WONDERS,' the voice
of an angel, the enigma of similitude and of

parable, all

the ALIEN that BESETS us here,—

. . . spoke not by them, but by HIMSELF,

calling us to return into that secret place from
which He

                    comes forth at last to us,—

. . . just as we two
together reached forth and for one

heartbeat attained to *TOUCH*

the *WISDOM* that is our *SOURCE* and *GROUND*,—

. . . if this could continue, and LIFE
were that one moment of
                    wisdom and understanding

for which we then sighed,—

would not *this* be: *ENTER THOU INTO THE JOY OF
     THY LORD?*

The first of these dependent clauses continues the expected pattern, moving from parsing through annotating

to end-stopped lines. But while the annotating lines have broken the syntax more aggressively than ever ("and of // parable, all // the ALIEN"), the effect of these line endings does not feel arbitrary: to make each dependent clause rise to a higher level of tension than the one preceding it, Bidart's lineation needs to become increasingly aggressive before it calms down again, preparing us for the beginning of the next dependent clause.

But the final dependent clause disrupts the pattern. It begins not with parsing lines but with line endings that immediately annotate the syntax: "and LIFE / were that one moment of / wisdom." At this point in our experience of the sentence, the disruption of the pattern now feels as exciting as the establishment of the pattern felt at the beginning of the sentence. By foreshortening the pattern, moving immediately into annotating lines, Bidart launches us into the final line of the sentence: the much-delayed independent clause, the payoff for our negotiation of this syntactical thicket.

> would not *this* be: *ENTER THOU INTO THE JOY OF THY LORD?*

Usually, the strategic delay of the subject in a periodic sentence makes its arrival feel momentous. But reduced to its simplest form, Bidart's sentence says something oddly tautological: "if we could hear the voice of God,

would it not say 'enter thou into the joy of thy Lord?'"
That's close to saying that if we could enter into the
joy of the Lord, then we could enter into the joy of the
Lord. And in itself, the insight is merely as interesting as the final line of Williams's "Pastoral" or Glück's
"Nostos." The whole sentence embodies a deeper wisdom: more devastating than whatever the voice of God
might say is the process we must negotiate in order
to hear what it says. Bidart's sentence is about sound,
but more profoundly, the sentence is itself the sound
of language organized in lines so that we might experience the sound as pleasure.

T. S. Eliot once said that poetry is a form of punctuation, and few poets embody that observation on the
page more strenuously than Bidart, who pushes punctuation, typography, and lineation to strategically ex-
pressive ends, forcing us to hear the movement of his
syntax in one way rather than in another way. But if his
use of punctuation and typography can seem idiosyncratic, his deployment of line is paradigmatic. Each line
of "Confessional" forces us to recognize the implications
of formal decisions that every poet makes with every
line he commits to paper—no matter what kind of line
or combination of lines the poet employs. To hear the
work of line in a great contemporary poem is to listen
again to the whole history of poetry in English.

Listen to one final poem—a poem that like Pound's

Hugh Selwyn Mauberley is organized in rhymed quatrains but that unlike *Mauberley* is not lineated on the page as rhymed quatrains.

> Experience is the Angled
> Road
> Preferred against the
> Mind
> By—Paradox—The
> Mind itself
> Presuming it to lead
>
> Quite opposite—How
> Complicate
> The Discipline of
> Man—
> Compelling Him to
> Choose Himself
> His Pre appointed Pain—

This is a transcription of the way Emily Dickinson lineated her poem on the page: while it does not capture the precise spacing of her words or the particular length and direction of her dashes, it does preserve her line endings, and the resulting lines do not correspond precisely to the poem's metrical pattern. In contrast, all available editions of her work print this poem in regular stanzas: rhymed quatrains of alternating tetrameter and trimeter lines.

Some readers will always maintain that Dickinson's line endings are simply produced by the collision of handwriting and margin, just as earlier readers maintained that her punctuation would have been corrected had she published her poems in conventional ways. Dickinson's practice varies too much to allow us to rest too comfortably on its conclusion, however: when setting down other poems, she altered the size of her handwriting to make the line fit the page. Early editors regularized Dickinson's idiosyncratic punctuation and irregular rhythms, and recent editions have restored many of these crucial aspects of Dickinson's rhythmic fingerprint while regularizing her lineation.

> Experience is the Angled Road
> Preferred against the Mind
> By—Paradox—the Mind itself
> Presuming it to lead

This lineation makes complete sense, since it reinforces our ability to hear the poem's alternating tetrameter and trimeter lines. But for ears educated by the line endings employed by Milton, Williams, or Bidart, Dickinson's original line endings also function aurally: the poet who employs punctuation with no grammatical function in order to create pauses and stresses that run against meter—

> By—Paradox—the Mind itself

—also harnesses the tension between syntax, meter, and line to control the rhythmic life of her poems.

> By—Paradox—The
> Mind itself

As is the case with Moore's multiple versions of "When I Buy Pictures," one doesn't know exactly how to choose. The dilemma is part of Dickinson's power, and it won't ever be solved because Dickinson's power is bound up with the endlessly equivocal nature of line. What matters most is the dilemma itself, not any particular solution. The different lineations alter the pattern of stress created by the play between meter, rhyme, syntax, and line.

All four of these elements are in tension in Dickinson's poem, as they are in the rhymed quatrains of Pound's *Mauberley*. Three of them are in tension in Moore's poems, two of them in Williams's. How much can a great poem afford to give up? From the start, I've argued that the fluctuating tension between syntax and line is crucial to poetry at large, discovering it in

Shakespeare and Milton as well as Glück and Bidart. But there are poems that give up this tension almost completely: the prose poem strategically relinquishes the power of line in the same way that a blank-verse poem relinquishes the power of rhyme or a free-verse poem relinquishes the power of meter. We've seen that the play of meter and rhyme is often present in poems that are not regularly metered and rhymed, however, and line similarly continues to be crucial to poems that are not written in lines. This paradox is the springboard for the following chapter.

Poem and Prose

Whatever else he is, James Joyce is one of the great makers of lines in the English language.

> Bronze by gold heard the hoofirons, steelyringing.
> Imperthnthn thnthnthn.
> Chips, picking chips off rocky thumbnail, chips.
> Horrid! And gold flushed more.
> A husky fifenote blew.
> Blew. Blue bloom is on the.
> Goldpinnacled hair.
> A jumping rose on satiny breast of satin, rose of Castile.
> Trilling, trilling: Idolores
> Peep! Who's in the . . . . peepofgold?
> Tink cried to bronze in pity.
> And a call, pure, long and throbbing. Longindying call.
> Decoy. Soft word. But look: the bright stars fade. Notes
>   chirruping answer.
> O rose! Castile. The moon is breaking.
> Jingle jingle jaunted jingling.
> Coin rang. Clock clacked.
> Avowal. *Sonnez.* I could. Rebound of garter. Not leave
>   thee. Smack. *La cloche!* Thigh smack. Avowal.
>   Warm. Sweetheart, goodbye! Jingle. Bloo.

> Boomed crashing chords. When love absorbs. War!
>   War! The tympanum.
> A sail! A veil awave upon the waves.
> Lost. Throstle fluted. All is lost now.

These are the opening twenty-one lines of the "Sirens" episode of Joyce's novel *Ulysses:* the episode continues in this fashion for another thirty-nine end-stopped lines until Joyce forsakes lineation for a kind of writing that looks like prose. Like Pound's end-stopped lines, these lines focus our attention on a variety of rhythmic and sonic patterns within the compass of the line. But unlike Pound's, the lines do not necessarily confirm syntactical closure. And unlike Moore's end-stopped lines, the lines do not organize our apprehension of a discursive argument. And unlike Whitman's end-stopped lines, the lines do not reinforce our awareness of repeated syntactical patterns. Instead, while Joyce's lines often end in a way that implies enjambment, the syntax does not continue in such a way that would make us experience the tension of enjambment: "Blew. Blue bloom is on the." Occasionally the lines end with an even more willful arbitrariness, as if to suggest that the syllables (even the surname of Joyce's protagonist, Leopold Bloom) exist as pure sound to be manipulated as such: "Jingle. Bloo."

The "Sirens" episode is about the seduction of sound. Leopold Bloom is nervously killing time in the bar of the Ormond Hotel at the precise moment when he suspects that his wife has arranged a sexual tryst. But when he catches a glimpse of the man he presumes to be Molly's lover, Bloom doesn't intervene; instead, he stays behind and listens to a group of drunken men sing songs. In what way is Bloom, Joyce's modern-day Odysseus, seduced by the music of the Sirens? In what way is the reader seduced by Joyce's effort to transform prose into medium that we read not in order to collect information but instead to savor its sonic pleasure?

The opening sixty lines of the "Sirens" episode are a condensation of the prose narrative that follows it: as we continue reading, we discover a context of narrative logic in which every line we've read, no matter how fragmentary, makes complete sense. For instance, the first line of the episode ("Bronze by gold heard the hoof-irons, steelyringing") is culled from the first sentence of the subsequent prose narrative, which describes two barmaids, one brunette, one blonde, listening to the viceregal cavalcade roll past the Ormond Hotel.

> Bronze by gold, miss Douce's head by miss Kennedy's head, over the crossblind of the Ormond bar heard the viceregal hoofs go by, ringing steel.

A page later, even the pure sound of the second line ("Imperthnthn thnthnthn") is revealed to be one character's mockery of another character's pronunciation of the phrase "impertinent insolence." In every case, what appears initially to be a fragment of sound is shown subsequently to be derived from complete and logical sentences. For Joyce, line is a way of making familiar language strange again.

But Joyce is not merely indulging in verbal high jinks.

> Boomed crashing chords. When love absorbs. War!
>   War! The tympanum.
> A sail! A veil awave upon the waves.
> Lost. Throstle fluted. All is lost now.

These lines offer snatches from songs that are sung in the Ormond Bar, the most important of which is "All is lost" or "Tutto è sciolto," from Bellini's *La Sonnambula.* In the opera, the heroine innocently sleepwalks her way into a situation that appears to be a sexual assignation; her fiancé believes that all is lost. In the "Sirens" episode, Leopold Bloom also believes that all is lost, that his wife is unfaithful. But Joyce suggests that Bloom ought to pay attention to the meaning of the words he hears: rather than listening to the aria "All is lost" as pure sound, ripped from the context of the opera's narrative, he should entertain the possibility that he too is mistaken about his wife.

Similarly, Joyce suggests that readers of *Ulysses* ought not to forget narrative context even when language is made to seem like nothing but sound. Of course the seduction of sound is paramount; poetry cannot exist without it. But we ignore the seduction of plain sense, Joyce suggests, at our own peril. The pleasure of *Ulysses* is that Joyce takes neither of these seductions for granted, forcing us to become aware of the kind of work we do when making sense of any linguistic utterance. Words mean something because they always threaten to sound like something else.

We are used to thinking of prose poetry as writing that sacrifices lineation in order to partake more readily of certain aspects of prose: our attention shifts from line to sentence, and syntax must hold our attention without the additional direction of line (or meter or rhyme). In contrast, the opening passage of "Sirens" is prose that has sacrificed syntactical and narrative closure in order to partake more readily of certain aspects of poetry: our attention shifts from sentence to line, and sonic patterns must hold our attention without the additional direction of sentences that satisfy our hunger for predication. In either case, there is no firm division to be made between the varieties of lineated poetry and the varieties of what we refer to more murkily as prose poetry. The effect of Joyce's "Sirens" depends on the introduction of lineation into the formal decorum of prose. The effect of our more typical notion of a prose poem depends on the deletion of lineation from the formal decorum of poetry, and the absence of the line would not be interesting if we did not feel the possibility of its presence.

Listen to the conclusion of John Ashbery's prose poem "Retro."

The midnight forest drags you along, thousands of peach hectares. Told him I wouldn't do it if I was him. Nothing to halt the chatter of locusts until they're put away for the night. He edges closer to your locker. Why did I leave it open? I've forgotten the combination. But it seems he's not interested in the locker, maybe my shoe—something unlike anything he's ever known. Sensing the tension he broke the ice with a quip about the weather somewhere, or maybe— maybe an observation on time, how it moves vastly in different channels, always keeping up with itself, until the day—I'm going to drive back to the office, a fellowship of miles, collect some of last year's ammunition. Then I'm definitely going to the country, he laughs.

Nine sentences, the first of which establishes a scene and a mode of address ("The midnight forest drags you along"), the second of which seems unrelated to the scene and disrupts the mode, turning from the second person to a first-person account of a third person ("Told him I wouldn't do it if I was him"). The next sentence returns to the outdoor scene ("chatter of locusts"), but the following sentences establish a new scene, the interior of a school building. And while these sentences don't turn away from the new scene, they mix up the modes of address: "He edges closer to your locker. Why did I leave it open? I've forgotten the combination." Here, the "you" addressed at the beginning of the passage has merged with the "I" who first addressed the "you." Then, when the eighth and longest sentence returns to the first person after beginning in the third person, the "I" doesn't seem to be the same "I" who spoke earlier: instead, the "he" who edged toward the locker now seems to be speaking: "I'm going to drive back to the office, a fellowship of miles, collect some of last year's ammunition. Then I'm definitely going to the country, he laughs."

This passage looks like prose, but it invokes the narrative logic we associate with prose while at the same time dismantling it. There's a whisper of continuity to these phrases ("drive back to the office"—"collect some of last year's ammunition"—"going to the country"), since one might imagine a reason for collecting the ammunition at the office before heading to the country. But the narrative links are suppressed, and the real pleasure of the passage lies in the way it leaps from one register of diction to another: the office, the ammunition, the country. Rather than fulfilling the expectations aroused by narrative logic, the passage foregrounds the disjunctive movement we associate more readily with poetry and in particular with lineated poetry.

Think of the way Joyce's end-stopped lines follow on each other in "Sirens." Or think of the way the final line of James Wright's "Lying in a Hammock at William Duffy's Farm in Pine Island, Minnesota" leaps from the lines preceding it.

> I lean back, as the evening darkens and comes on.
> A chicken hawk floats over, looking for home.
> I have wasted my life.

Here, the movement from descriptive lines to the final moralizing line feels ironic; we suspect that Wright doesn't really mean that he's wasted his life, or we feel a need to reconsider the virtue of wasting one's life altogether. In contrast, the end of Ashbery's "Retro" feels even more challengingly ambiguous, less clearly ironic, because of the many different and contradictory leaps that have taken place both between and within the sentences. The freedom extolled in the poem's final sentence ("Then I'm definitely going to the country, he laughs") is embodied in the poem's disruption of the continuity of scene, diction, and address.

What's more, the formal configuration of "Retro" seems to embody this flight from constraint: for while the poem concludes with the prose passage I've quoted so far, the first half of the poem is organized in lines. Here, Ashbery controls pacing and intonation through the kind of interplay of different line endings that we've observed in poets from Shakespeare to Bidart—an interplay that becomes even more crucial in poetry that privileges sonic over semantic coherence.

> It's really quite a thrill
> when the moon rises above the hill
> and you've gotten over someone
> salty and mercurial, the only person you ever loved.
>
> Walks in the park are enjoyed.

The first two lines, marked by rhyme, parse the syntax ("a thrill / when"; "the hill / and"). Then the third line annotates it ("someone / salty"), pushing us into the fourth line while the final syllable of the word "mercurial" pulls us back by recalling the opening rhyme. The fourth line itself is end-stopped, and, after the stanza division, the fifth line is not only end-stopped but syntactically complete. Reading the passage, regardless of what it says, we experience the sound of an argument accumulating sense, a steady increase in the tension between syntax and line giving way to the stasis of confirmation: "Walks in the park are enjoyed." Listen to the rest of the lineated portion of the poem.

Going to Jerusalem now
I walked into a hotel room.
I didn't need a name or anything.
I went to Bellevue Hospital,
got a piece of the guy.
As I say, it's really quite a thrill.

Quite a thrill too to bend objects
that always return to their appointed grooves—
will it be always thus? Or will auto parts
get to have their day in the sun?

Got to drone now.
Princess Ida plans to overwork us four days a week
until the bracts have mauved up.
Then it's a tailgate party—
how would you like your burger done?

A little tea with that?

I saw her wailing for some animals.
That doesn't mean a thing doesn't happen
Or only goes away, or gets worse.
What's the worst that could happen?

The plain sense of these lines is more readily available than the sense of the prose passage that follows them: "Retro" is about the feeling of having been released from the fetters of prior experience. If we must work hard for four days, we can nonetheless look forward to the tailgate party. If we've lost the only person we've ever loved, we can nonetheless enjoy casual sex. We don't even need a name. If the work of bending objects "to their appointed grooves" once seemed thrilling, we can nonetheless look forward to the moment when objects might seem gloriously lacking in their previously appointed purpose. This wisdom applies both to auto parts, which might be yanked from the whole machine to glisten in the sun, and to sentences, which might be allowed to wander from the lines of a poem. "What's the worst that could happen?" asks the last line that appears in "Retro," and the answer is the passage of nine unlineated sentences with which the poem concludes. Formally as well as thematically, this poem heads for the open road.

Or does it? What about the tone of Ashbery's poem? Is "Retro" merely suggesting that walks in the park and one-night stands are to be preferred to the memory of the only person we've ever loved? That automobiles ought to be dismantled, their parts splayed across the lawn so we can recognize their true beauty? That we'll be happier if we give up the fetters of lineation and wallow in prose? That we'll be happier still if we forsake the narrative logic we associate with prose? That freedom can automatically be purchased at the expense of constraint?

It may be thrilling to consider what might happen to our sentences when we stop thinking about lines, just as it may be thrilling to consider what might happen to our lines when we stop thinking about meter and rhyme. But to say that such relinquishments are "really quite a thrill," as the opening line of "Retro" does, is to highlight the self-satisfaction that may too easily accompany such relinquishments. The very shape of Ashbery's "Retro" (a poem that begins in lines and ends in prose) suggests that we inevitably think about lineation when we read a prose poem, just as we think about the whole car when we admire the beauty of auto parts. Ashbery is not asking us to choose between different ways of organizing language in a poem: he wants to liberate us from a too-familiar narrative of what constitutes our liberation. He wants to liberate us from the tyranny of risk as we have learned to recognize it.

Some poets have argued that the rejection of line carries a kind of political charge, just as poets once felt that the rejection of rhyming verse for blank verse or blank verse for free verse carried a political charge. This may be true in a particular time at a particular place. But it cannot be true categorically. For example, even if the heroic couplet was once associated with hierarchical thinking in the eighteenth century, it does not follow that the heroic couplet will always inevitably be doomed to reproduce the same hierarchies in our thought. The relationship between formal choice and ideological position is constantly shifting, and it isn't possible to predict the repercussions of formal decisions except inasmuch as we might see them played out in the work of individual poets.

In certain circumstances, consequently, the rejection of line may be liberating or it may be constricting. In other circumstances, the adoption of line may be liberating or constricting. If a poet who works in lines feels that her syntax isn't very interesting, abandoning lines may allow her to discover syntactical possibilities that her usual manner of lineation has occluded. And if a poet who has abandoned lines finds that her syntax has grown predictable, then the introduction of lineation may provide a tension that will reinvigorate the syntax.

Think back to William Carlos Williams. In poems like the early "Pastoral," Williams was wedded to the parsing line, a line that in Williams's hands tends to grow flaccid because it so consistently breaks the syntax into its predictable parts. But by the time he published *Spring and All*, Williams had added the annotating line to his poetic tool kit, a line that cuts against the already plain parameters of syntax. His syntax itself became more varied, his range of diction grew wider, and his tendency to close his poems with ready-made wisdom was sharply curtailed.

Many things, including the example of Marianne Moore's syllabic poems, fueled this transformation, but in the few years that passed between "Pastoral" and *Spring and All*, Williams wrote a collection of prose poems called *Kora in Hell*, and in retrospect it's easy to see why the relinquishment of lineation not only produced dazzling writing in itself but ultimately transformed Williams's relationship to the poetic line.

Talk as you will, say: "No woman wants to bother with children in this country";—speak of your Amsterdam and the whitest aprons and brightest doorknobs in Christendom. And I'll answer you: Gleaming doorknobs and scrubbed entries have heard the songs of the housemaids at sun-up and—housemaids are wishes. Whose? Ha! the dark canals are whistling, whistling for who will cross to the other side. If I remain with hands in pocket leaning upon my lamppost—why—I

bring curses to a hag's lips and her daughter on her
arm knows better than I can tell you—best to blush
and out with it than back beaten after.

Five sentences, the shortest of which consists of one
syllable ("Whose?"), a question that confirms the reader's growing disorientation, the longest of which crams
together three clauses, first with a conjunction ("and
her daughter") and then with a dash ("—best to blush").
The rhythmic vitality of the final clause is so acute, its
stressed syllables so artfully reinforced by alliteration,
that it begs to be scanned—

> BEST to BLUSH and OUT with IT than BACK
> > BEATen AFTer

—but the connection of this clause to the clauses preceding it feels both grammatically and semantically
tenuous. Like Ashbery's, Williams's prose poem privileges sonic over semantic coherence, flirting with narrative logic only to make us feel its fragility.

But while Ashbery begs the question of prose poetry's relationship to poetry by moving from lineated to
unlineated sentences, Williams asks us to consider prose
poetry's relationship to prose: he follows his prose poem
with a prose commentary, and the commentary emphasizes narrative links that the prose poem suppresses.

> *In Holland at daybreak, of a fine spring morning, one sees the housemaids beating rugs before the small houses of such a city as Amsterdam, sweeping, scrubbing the low entry steps and polishing doorbells and doorknobs. By night perhaps there will be an old woman with a girl on her arm, histing and whistling across a deserted canal to some late loiterer trudging aimlessly on beneath the gas lamps.*

These sentences present Williams's point more plainly: the civic decorum of the Dutch city disguises its more lascivious nightlife. But if this thematic perspicuity adds something to our experience of the prose poem, it also takes something away. For while the prose commentary proposes a neat opposition between daylight cleanliness and nighttime lasciviousness, the prose poem allows us to entertain the notion that doorknob-scrubbing housemaids are themselves an expression of the wish for darkness: the more disorderly verbal decorum adds complexity to Williams's point.

In addition, the suppression of narrative logic in the prose poem encourages Williams to listen to his language, liberating him to take pleasure in counterintuitive leaps (doorknobs that hear songs, canals that are whistling) and allowing him to produce sentences with greater rhythmic interest: "Gleaming doorknobs and scrubbed entries have heard the songs of the housemaids at sun-up." To think about lineating the commentary is to think about parceling out its sense—

> In Holland at daybreak,
> of a fine spring morning,
> one sees the housemaids beating rugs
> before the small houses

—but to think about lineating the prose poem is to stop thinking so much about sense and to start listening to patterns of rhythmic stress and sonic echo within the syntax.

> Best to blush and
> out with it than back
> beaten after.

This is what Williams did when he followed the prose poems of *Kora in Hell* with the lineated poems of *Spring and All:* writing prose revitalized the syntax of the poems, and the new syntax demanded that Williams explore a wider variety of line endings, moving away from his more predictable dependence on the parsing line.

"There is no such thing as prose," said Stéphane Mallarmé. "There is the alphabet, and then there are verses which are more or less closely knit, more or less diffuse. So long as there is a straining toward style, there is versification." This statement is not merely provocative. Williams needed to write logical prose so that he might hear what disjunctive prose could sound like, just as he needed to write unlineated sentences in order to hear what lines could sound like. He placed the two kinds of prose side by side in *Kora in Hell* so that we might feel the necessity of his excursion from lineated poetry, just as Ashbery wedged prose poetry against lineated poetry in "Retro" so that we might hear how one formal gesture invokes, depends on, complicates the other. Truly to strain toward style, to write in one way rather than another way, is not to take a stand on prose or line or meter or rhyme: it is to discover what the language of a particular poem requires.

What do these sentences require? How might they strain toward style?

> How should the world gain if this house failed, even though a hundred little houses were the better for it, for here power [has] gone forth or lingered, giving energy, precision; it gave to a far people beneficent rule, and still under its roof living intellect is sweetened by old memories of its descent from far off? How should the world be better if the wren's nest flourish and the eagle's house is scattered?

William Butler Yeats wrote these sentences in his journal on the morning of August 7, 1909. As the passage suggests, Yeats had a lot of ideas for poems. He was passionately concerned about a number of social issues, but he hadn't written much poetry in years. He worried that his ideas were themselves the problem. Later the same day, however, Yeats wrote down this line—

How should the world be better if this house

—a pentameter line derived from the opening phrase of the prose passage: "How should the world gain if this house failed." That phrase could also be a pentameter, though a slightly clunkier one. By substituting the phrase "be better" for "gain," Yeats smoothed out the iambs and pushed the main verb to the next line, creating an enjambment that moves the poem forward. He retained the line's opening trochee ("HOW should"), taking advantage of the misplaced accent's call to attention. Then, reconsidering the word "better," he changed it to "luckier," roughening up his pentameter in a different way by adding an extra unstressed syllable.

How should the world be luckier if this house

Finally, Yeats continued his new sentence through six additional pentameter lines, delaying the verb we expect at the beginning of the second line until the middle of the third line. When he got to the third line, he jettisoned his original verb ("failed") in favor of the more tactile "became too ruinous," which also had the advantage of rhyming in an attractively off-key way with "house."

> How should the world be luckier if this house
> Where passion and precision have been one
> Time out of mind became too ruinous
> To breed the lidless eye that loves the sun
> And the sweet laughing eagle thoughts that grow
> Where wings have memory of wings and all
> That comes of the best knit to the best?

These lines are very close to the final version of "Upon a House Shaken by the Land Agitation"; only the punctuation would be changed. The second and fourth lines are fairly regular pentameters, but like the first line, the third begins with an inverted foot ("TIME out of MIND"), and the fifth begins with an extra unaccented syllable ("And the SWEET"). The cumulative effect is that his syntax creates a rhythmic pattern but at the same time deviates from it enough to make the syntax feel under tension, determined to move through the pattern.

At the same time, a rhyme scheme has taken shape: A B A B C D—then what? The seventh line could have ended where the syntax ends, giving these seven lines a satisfying moment of closure; but as it stands, the seventh line contains only four stresses, not the required five.

That COMES of the BEST KNIT to the BEST?

Yeats needed another iamb rhyming with "grow," and he could have written something like "That comes of the best knit to the best we've known." Instead, he added the word "although" ("That comes of the best knit to the best? Although") and moved immediately into the unbroken syntactical swoop of the poem's concluding five lines.

> Although
> Mean roof-trees were the sturdier for its fall,
> How should their luck run high enough to reach
> The gifts that govern men, and after these
> To gradual Time's last gift, a written speech
> Wrought of high laugher, loveliness and ease?

The spell was broken. By turning to prose, then casting his prose into lines, Yeats was writing some of his greatest poetry after several years of having written almost none.

While he often wrote highly figurative and rhythmic prose, following the examples of Walter Pater and Mallarmé, Yeats was never inclined to write prose poetry. But whenever he wrote out a prose version of what he imagined a poem might be, the poem became itself not because of the logical sense of the prose but because

a snatch of language in the prose ignited, leading soni-
cally to other words, creating patterns of sound while simultaneously disrupting them. Writing "Upon a House
Shaken by the Land Agitation," Yeats first worried about
having a discursive argument at all, because he knew that
the argument not only wouldn't make a poem but might
inhibit the making of a poem. Then he wrote down the
argument anyway. Then he listened to what he had written, liberated from the known world of conviction into
the mysterious, unmade world of sound. Like Williams
and Ashbery, Yeats privileges sonic coherence.

Still, we don't have much trouble following the sense
of Yeats's poem, as we might when first encountering
Williams's prose poem. But we probably don't enter the
experience of Yeats's poem because we want to know
what it says about the rent reductions imposed on land
owners by the Irish courts—just as we are probably
not motivated to read Williams's prose poem in order
to glean his thoughts about Dutch morality. We enter
the experience of "Upon a House Shaken by the Land
Agitation" because we are seduced by the tensions between the underlying pentameter and the rhythms of
the syntax, between the rhythms of the syntax and the
length of the lines as they are marked by the rhyme
scheme.

Beginning with my discussion of the speech from
Shakespeare's *King Lear*, I have stressed the impor-

tance of these tensions: the effect of the line is unpredictable except inasmuch as a particular line interacts with the other elements of a particular poem. But the only plausible proscription in art is that there can be no proscriptions. Yeats's prose sentences become more vital when they are recast in lines. Williams's lineation becomes more complex by virtue of his abandonment of lines. Finally, the very nature of line encourages us to question the power of line. For if it's not possible to predict the effect of any particular kind of line except in its relationship to syntax, then we will inevitably come to consider the effect of suppressing that tension. Meter and rhyme provoke us similarly.

What remains to be relinquished? If syntax shoulders more weight in the absence of line, what happens to syntax if we jettison punctuation as well? Joyce did so famously at the end of *Ulysses,* offering an entire chapter of unpunctuated prose.

and O that awful deepdown torrent O and the sea the sea crimson sometimes like fire and the glorious sunsets and the figtrees in the Alameda gardens yes and all the queer little streets and the pink and blue and yellow houses and the rosegardens and the jessamine and geraniums and cactuses and Gibraltar as a girl where I was a Flower of the mountain yes when I put the rose in my hair like the Andalusian girls used or

shall I wear a red yes and how he kissed me under the
Moorish wall and I thought well as well him as another and then I asked him with my eyes to ask again
yes and then he asked me would I yes to say yes my
mountain flower and first I put my arms around him
yes and drew him down to me so he could feel my
breasts all perfume yes and his heart was going like
mad and yes I said yes I will Yes.

Here, no matter how obscure the connections between
his clauses and phrases, Joyce lures us forward by em-
phasizing other qualities we think of when we call prose
poetic: luxuriously concrete diction (drawing attention to individual clauses and phrases rather than the
grammatical links between them) and a steady pulse of
repeated syllables (linking clauses and phrases whose
relationship may be grammatically tenuous). In addition, however complex the syntax within the clauses,
the connections between the clauses are simply paratac-
tic. And when syntactical ambiguity does erupt, the ambiguity functions psychologically: weaving this endless
sentence, Molly Bloom conflates her former lovers with
her husband (Bloom asked her to say yes, but another
man kissed her under the Moorish wall). The slippage
between the past and the present allows Molly to affirm
her ongoing life in the future: in a sense, she can't live
with punctuation.

In "Idem 4," Michael Palmer suggests that we all live without punctuation all the time. This section of his unpunctuated prose poem nods to Molly's "yes," but rather than linking the clauses paratactically, as Joyce does, Palmer gathers them together in one giant independent clause.

> now I say yes to the bridge the dead cross no thicker than a fingernail no wider than a knife eyes fixed on the Gates of Paradise yes to the visible hills the actual hills olive trees with grey underleaf commas between each breath brief tremor smell of gunpowder then screams it was screams and screams all the way through

Here, the opening clause ("Now I say yes to") governs everything that follows: the bridge that the dead cross, the visible hills, the olive trees on the hills, the smell of gunpowder, the screams. And once again the syntactical ambiguity feels functional, especially since it builds as the poem progresses: in this run-on vision of heaven, punctuation exists on the other side of the river, where there are "commas between each breath."

Unpunctuated prose is rare, however, and the unpunctuated prose poem is even more uncommon. In contrast, it's revealing to remember that unpunctuated poetry has a long and rich history: lineation may

compensate for or take advantage of the lack of punctuation in various ways. In prose poetry, the persistence
of punctuation is an acknowledgment of the power of
line. And in unpunctuated poetry, line is an acknowledgment of the power of punctuation, which is to say
syntax. Listen to the opening lines of C. D. Wright's
"Various Positions."

It was getting on toward suppertime

It was his night off

A shoe dropped

It had nothing whatsoever to do with you

It was an efficiency apartment

The breast seeks its own level

The table got down on its knees

With an amaryllis at their sill

They assume late spring donkey

It was stifling

It is the hair that makes it so mysterious

A book of matches goes off in her shirt

With one exception, these one-line stanzas are syntactically complete, and their syntax is so simple that we don't require any punctuation to follow their sense. The punctuated lines from the beginning of Joyce's "Sirens" are all end-stopped as well, but they nonetheless give the impression of enjambment because of the way Joyce deploys the line to fragment the syntax: "Blue bloom is on the." In contrast, Wright's poem feels provocatively static, arranged in lines that don't seem to function as lines in relationship to the syntax. Like a prose poem, a poem written in syntactically closed lines suppresses the work of the line, focusing our attention on the sentence or sentence fragment.

Wright's title obviously refers to the sexual overtones of her poem's subject matter, but it also alerts us to the subtly different ways in which she is in fact positioning her line in relationship to her syntax: as it moves forward, the poem does not simply substitute line endings for punctuation but takes strategic advantage of the lack of punctuation. The first seven lines of "Various Positions" are end-stopped in a particular way; syntax equals line, and there is no suggestion of syntactical continuity between one line and the next. But the one syntactically incomplete line is a prepositional phrase ("With an amaryllis at their sill"), and the line parses the phrase so that we assume a syntactical continuity between the eighth line and the ninth, the plural possessive ("their") preparing us for the subject of the independent clause ("they").

> With an amaryllis at their sill
>
> They assume late spring donkey

At first, this break from the poem's stern sequence of end-stopped lines seems like an exception rather than a structural shift: the poem returns immediately to its initial decorum of syntactically complete end-stopped lines. But toward the end of the poem we encounter two more parsing lines, both of them prepositional phrases as well.

> He wants nothing more than to sleep
>
> Inside her holster
>
> The chair fell to pieces
>
> On the eve of the eighth day
>
> Her milk came in

These two prepositional phrases ("Inside her holster" and "On the eve of the eighth day") work differently than the first one we encountered ("With an amaryllis at the sill"). Now, we are at greater liberty to read the syntax in two different ways, depending on the independent clause to which we link the preposition. First, we read the syntax this way.

> He wants nothing more than to sleep
>
> Inside her holster

Then, we are also encouraged to link the prepositional phrase to the following line—

> Inside her holster
>
> The chair fell to pieces

—except that while this sentence is syntactically coherent, it is semantically incoherent. Finally, when we reach the last of the poem's three parsing lines, the effect of the continuing syntax is altered once again, for now the two ways of reading the relationship of the lines are syntactically as well as semantically coherent: we may choose between this reading of the syntax—

The chair fell to pieces

On the eve of the eighth day

—and this reading of the syntax.

On the eve of the eighth day

Her milk came in

This effect is not in itself uncommon. Emily Dickinson sometimes fosters the same kind of syntactical ambiguity by eschewing conventional punctuation between her lines. And at moments of great dramatic tension, George Oppen creates this slippage not only between the lines but within the lines, momentarily refusing to organize his syntax with either punctuation or lineation.

> help me I am
of that people the grass

blades touch

and touch in their small

distances the poem
begins

This effect is not in itself complex: few formal strategies are. But because Oppen begins "If It All Went Up in Smoke" by parsing syntax with his lines, the eruption of run-on syntax feels exciting rather than merely confusing. Similarly, in "Various Positions," a poem that begins by sternly curtailing the work of lineation while also jettisoning punctuation, Wright's movement between three different ways of deploying a simple parsing line feels revelatory—the embodiment of the momentous physical transformation that the final line of the poem describes. We're used to poems moving from discursive continuity to surprising moments of disjunction; this is the thrill of the concluding line of James Wright's "Lying in a Hammock at William Duffy's Farm." In contrast, C. D. Wright energizes the opposite movement, making the simplest gesture of narrative continuity seem astonishing again: "On the eve of the eighth day / Her milk came in."

Whatever shape it takes, this kind of movement is what makes a poem feel like an act of discovery rather than an act of recitation—an event that happens on the page rather than a recounting of an event that happened prior to the page. Lineation is a powerful tool for creating such movement, but not because a poet chooses simply to write pentameter lines or syntactically complete lines or no lines at all. What matters within any particular formal decorum is variation: the making of pattern along with the simultaneous disruption of pattern. It's not the pentameter that matters as such in the speech from *King Lear* but the way in which we move within the blank verse from end-stopped lines to enjambed lines. It's not Ashbery's decision to write narrative prose that matters in "Retro" but his slow disruption of the terms of narrative logic. And it's not Wright's decision to reduce the power of line but her strategic relaxation of what initially seems like an unalterable decision. This kind of movement—the establishment of a formal decorum in which even the smallest variation from it feels thrilling—is what makes the act of reading a poem feel like the act of writing a poem. It is what makes a poem an experience we need to have more than once, an act of discovery that is contingent not simply upon what we learn but on the temporal process of discovering how it feels to learn again what we've always known.

Listen, in conclusion, to one last passage of prose.

To complain of the fascination of what's difficult. It spoils spontaneity and pleasure and it wastes time. Repeat the line ending "difficult" three times, and rhyme on bolt, exult, colt, jolt. One could use the thought of the wild-winged and unbroken colt [that] must drag a cart of stones out of pride because it's difficult, and end by denouncing drama, accounts, public contests—all that's merely difficult.

Yeats wrote these sentences in his journal several months after completing "Upon a House Shaken by the Land Agitation." Once again, he is in search of a poem; this paragraph is the seedbed for "The Fascination of What's Difficult." But what had earlier been a groping in the dark has become a little bit like a method. For even as Yeats puts down this subject for a poem, he is already thinking more about the sound of the word "difficult" than about its meaning. He can hear the poem unfolding before he knows anything about its argument, structure, or form.

After waiting a few more months, Yeats set down two sentences cast in eight pentameter lines: the phrase "the fascination of what's difficult" became the opening pentameter, and the poem went on to rhyme "difficult" with "colt" and "jolt."

> The fascination of what's difficult
> Has dried the sap out of my veins and rent
> Spontaneous joy and natural content
> Out of my heart. There is something ails our colt
> That must, as if it had not holy blood
> Nor on Olympus leaped from cloud to cloud[,]
> Shiver at the lash, and strain and sweat and jolt
> As though it dragged road metal.

This is not the whole poem but, once again, this lineated draft is very close to the final version. The placement of the stressed syllables would be rearranged in the seventh line, making its conclusion punchier. Although we might scan the resulting pentameter of the final verson of the poem this way—

SHIVer UNder the LASH, strain, SWEAT and JOLT

—we are more apt to hear the line this way, the stressed syllables packed together—

SHIVer under the LASH, STRAIN, SWEAT and
    JOLT

—as they are in the following line as well.

As though it DRAGGED ROAD METal.

Yeats has solidified the rhythmic life of the poem, but once again, as was the case with the early draft of "Upon a House Shaken by the Land Agitation," this line is too short: it needs two more stresses to complete the pentameter. Once again, a rhyme scheme has taken shape: A B B A C C A, where the B and C rhymes ("rent" and "blood") are enticingly close to the original A rhyme ("difficult").

In "Upon a House Shaken by the Land Agitation," Yeats filled out the short line with the word "although," rhyming strongly with an earlier line, but here he does something more startling. He ends the line with a word that sounds nothing like any of the previous rhymes: "My curse on plays." As a result, the relationship between the first and second halves of the eighth line of "The Fascination of What's Difficult" is as deliciously disjunctive as the relationship between most of the lines in Wright's "Various Positions."

As though it dragged road metal

My curse on plays

Where is this poem going? Why would a poem with such a perspicuous argument so deftly lure us astray?

By suddenly expanding the palate of his rhyme scheme, shifting our ears to a strategically different sound, Yeats also discovers a structure for the poem, one that was familiar to him from thousands of Petrarchan sonnets, in which the first eight lines (or octet) offer a proposition on which the second six lines (or sestet) turn. But since Yeats has placed his volta (or turn) in the middle of the eighth line rather than at the beginning of the ninth line, where it traditionally appears, his thirteen-line poem has the structure of a sonnet but not the form of a sonnet. That is, the poem's argument turns against itself as a sonnet's argument turns, but the proportions are just slightly off; the argument does not inhabit the meter and rhyme scheme in precisely the traditional fashion.

> My curse on plays
> That have to be set up in fifty ways,
> On the day's war with every knave and dolt,
> Theatre business, management of men.
> I swear before the dawn comes round again
> I'll find the stable and pull out the bolt.

Formally, this is not a true sestet, but it functions like one, turning sharply against the lines preceding it and concluding with two lines that have the rhetorical weight of a couplet but are not rhymed as a couplet: "I swear before the dawn comes round again / I'll find the stable and pull out the bolt." Yeats has simultaneously invoked a pattern and strayed from it.

If pressed, most anyone would say that "The Fascination of What's Difficult" is about Yeats's frustration with running the Abbey Theatre, one of the tasks that had kept him from the lyric poetry he wanted to write. But Yeats's initial prose version of the poem says almost nothing about theater business: drama appears in a list of possible subjects along with accounts and public contests. Instead, the prose draft sketches out rhymes that appear both before and after this pseudo sonnet's volta: difficult, colt, jolt, dolt, bolt. By searching for rhymes for the word "difficult," Yeats produced the metaphor of the winged colt who must be liberated from his stall. Then, the strategic disruption of these rhymes produced the poem's most thrillingly disjunctive moment: "My curse on plays." This phrase sounds as if it comes out of nowhere, as if the poem is discovering itself at the precise moment we are reading it.

Which is what every great poem does. Whatever else he is, Yeats is one of the great poets of the English language—but not because he writes in lines that are metered and rhymed. The opening passage of the "Sirens" chapter of *Ulysses* cautions us not to idealize the sound of language: Leopold Bloom is seduced by the sound of a song whose meaning could help him to make better sense of his life, and Joyce seduces us with what seems like the pure sound of words, only to show us that words have meanings to which we must attend. Approaching the same point from the opposite direction, Yeats's poems caution us not to idealize the meaning of language. Both "Upon a House by the Land Agitation" and "The Fascination of What's Difficult" have clearly paraphrasable arguments, but the arguments in themselves cannot produce a poem. Yeats's ear produces the poem. And when we reproduce the poem in our own ears, we are learning to listen to language that once threatened to make sense too surely.

Poems are poems because we want to listen to them. Some poems have a prominent argument; some poems don't. But all poems live or die on their capacity to lure us from their beginnings to their ends by a pattern of sounds. This is why a poem we don't understand may seem wonderfully satisfying, and this is why a poem we understand all too well may also seem wonderfully satisfying. A poem may harness the power of meter, rhyme, syntax, and line to establish and disrupt a pattern of sounds, and a poem may with equal integrity reject the power of meter, rhyme, syntax, and line. But the poet needs to understand what she is rejecting as well as what she is harnessing. Every poem is based at least implicitly on a choice to do something rather than something else, and, as a result, every poem takes power from its exclusions as well as its inclusions. Poetry is the sound of language organized in lines, I said at the beginning of this book. If that statement once seemed provocative, I hope it now seems like old news. Only a great poem could make it interesting again.

Further Reading

While line is implicitly a part of any discussion of prosody, it is not often accorded explicit or lengthy attention. The three finest exceptions to this observation may be found in Robert Pinsky's *The Sounds of Poetry: A Brief Guide*, Mary Kinzie's *A Poet's Guide to Poetry*, and Charles O. Hartman's *Free Verse: An Essay on Prosody*. Each of these books offers a distinctive discussion of line, but the arguments are not programmatic. The goal in each case is to describe a variety of poetic practices.

More specialized discussions of line may be found in Ellen Bryant Voigt's superb essay on syntax ("Syntax: Rhythm of Thought, Rhythm of Song") and in Susan Howe's groundbreaking essay on Emily Dickinson's manuscripts ("These Flames and Generosities of the Heart: Emily Dickinson and the Illogic of Sumptuary Values"). The interview in Frank Bidart's *In the Western Night: Collected Poems, 1965–90* includes brief but very provocative remarks on lineation. So does Allen Grossman's *Summa Lyrica*.

Less focused on line as such but still relevant to the discussion are Hugh Kenner's "Rhyme," a surprising history of the practice of rhyme in European languages, Stephen Fredman's *Poet's Prose*, the subtlest available account of prose poetry, and John Thompson's *The Founding of English Metre*, a book whose title does not do justice to the wide-ranging implications of its argument.

Interesting accounts of line may also be found in T. S. Eliot's "Reflections on *Vers Libre*," Donald Justice's "The Free-Verse Line in Stevens," Denise Levertov's "On the Function of the Line," and Charles Olson's "Projective Verse." Eliot's and Olson's essays have been especially influential; rather than offering a balanced account of line, they are themselves a part of the history of thinking about line in American poetry. Many of the essays collected in *The Line in Postmodern Poetry*, edited by Robert Frank and Henry Sayre, are also worth reading.

References

Ashbery, John. "Retro." In *Where Shall I Wander*, pp. 31–32. New York: HarperCollins, 2005.

Bidart, Frank. "Confessional." In *In the Western Night: Collected Poems, 1965–90*, pp. 53–74. New York: Farrar, Straus and Giroux, 1990.

———. "An Interview—With Mark Halliday." In *In the Western Night: Collected Poems, 1965–90*, pp. 223–41. New York: Farrar, Straus and Giroux, 1990.

Blake, William. "The Book of Thel." In *Complete Writings*, edited by Geoffrey Keynes, pp. 127–30. New York: Oxford University Press, 1976.

Cunningham, J. V. "How Shall the Poem be Written?" In *Collected Essays*, pp. 256–71. Chicago: Swallow Press, 1976.

Dickinson, Emily. "Experience is the Angled Road." In *The Manuscript Books*, edited by R. W. Franklin, 2:1033. 2 vols. Cambridge, MA: Harvard University Press, 1981.

———. "Experience is the Angled Road." In *The Poems of Emily Dickinson: Variorum Edition*, edited by R. W. Franklin, 2:839. 3 vols. Cambridge, MA: Harvard University Press, 1998.

Eliot, T. S. *Complete Poems and Plays.* New York: Harcourt, Brace and World, 1971.

———. "Reflections on *Vers Libre*." In *To Criticize the Critic and Other Writings*, pp. 183–89. London: Faber and Faber, 1965.

Frank, Robert, and Henry Sayre, editors. *The Line in Post-modern Poetry*. Urbana: University of Illinois Press, 1988.

Fredman, Stephen. *Poet's Prose: The Crisis in American Verse*. Cambridge: Cambridge University Press, 1983.

Frost, Robert. "After Apple Picking." In *Collected Poems, Prose, and Plays*, edited by Richard Poirier and Mark Richardson, pp. 70–71. New York: Library of America, 1995.

Ginsberg, Allen. "Sunflower Sutra." In *Howl and Other Poems*, pp. 35–38. San Francisco: City Lights Books, 1959.

Glück, Louise. "Nostos." In *Meadowlands*, p. 43. Hopewell, NJ: Ecco, 1996.

Grossman, Allen. *Summa Lyrica*. In *The Sighted Singer: Two Works on Poetry for Readers and Writers*, pp. 205–374. Baltimore: Johns Hopkins University Press, 1992.

Hartman, Charles O. *Free Verse: An Essay on Prosody*. Evanston, IL: Northwestern University Press, 1996.

Herbert, George. "The Collar." In *The English Poems of George Herbert*, edited by C. A. Patrides, pp. 161–62. London: J. M. Dent, 1974.

Herrick, Robert. "Upon His Departure Hence." In *The Poems of Robert Herrick*, edited by L. C. Martin, p. 178. New York: Oxford University Press, 1965.

Hollander, John. "'Sense Variously Drawn Out': On English Enjambment." In *Vision and Resonance: Two Senses of Poetic Form*, pp. 91–116. New York: Oxford University Press, 1975.

Howard, Richard. "November, 1889." In *Inner Voices: Selected Poems, 1963–2003*, pp. 44–56. New York: Farrar, Straus and Giroux, 2004.

Howe, Susan. "These Flames and Generosities of the Heart:
    Emily Dickinson and the Illogic of Sumptuary Values." In
    *The Birth-mark: Unsettling the Wilderness in American
    Literary History,* pp. 131–53. Hanover, NH: University
    Press of New England, 1993.
Joyce, James. *Ulysses: The Corrected Text,* edited by Hans
    Walter Gabler. New York: Random House, 1986.
Justice, Donald. "The Free-Verse Line in Stevens." In *Oblivion:
    On Writers and Writing,* pp. 13–38. Ashland, OR: Story
    Line, 1998.
———. "Nostalgia and Complaint of the Grandparents." In
    New and Selected Poems, pp. 156–57. New York: Knopf,
    1995.
Kenner, Hugh. "Rhyme: An Unfinished Monograph." *Common
    Knowledge* 10 (Fall 2004): 377–425.
Kinzie, Mary. *A Poet's Guide to Poetry.* Chicago: University
    of Chicago Press, 1999.
Levertov, Denise. "On the Function of the Line." In *Light up
    the Cave,* pp. 61–69. New York: New Directions, 1981.
Mallarmé, Stéphane. "The Evolution of Literature." In *Selected
    Prose Poems, Essays, and Letters,* translated by Bradford
    Cook, pp. 18–24. Baltimore: Johns Hopkins University
    Press, 1956.
Milton, John. *Paradise Lost.* In *Complete Poems and
    Major Prose,* edited by Merritt Hughes, pp. 209–469.
    Indianapolis, IN: Odyssey, 1957.
Moore, Marianne. "The Fish." In *Becoming Marianne Moore:
    The Early Poems, 1907–1924,* edited by Robin G. Schulze,
    pp. 85–86. Berkeley and Los Angeles: University of
    California Press, 2002.

———. "The Past is the Present." In *Becoming Marianne Moore: The Early Poems, 1907–1924,* edited by Robin G. Schulze, p. 74. Berkeley and Los Angeles: University of California Press, 2002.

———. "When I Buy Pictures." In *Becoming Marianne Moore: The Early Poems, 1907–1924,* edited by Robin G. Schulze, p. 255. Berkeley and Los Angeles: University of California Press, 2002.

———. "When I Buy Pictures." In *Becoming Marianne Moore: The Early Poems, 1907–1924,* edited by Robin G. Schulze, p. 257. Berkeley and Los Angeles: University of California Press, 2002.

Olson, Charles. "Projective Verse." In *Selected Writings,* edited by Robert Creeley, pp. 15–26. New York: New Directions, 1951.

Oppen, George. "If It All Went Up in Smoke." In *New Collected Poems,* edited by Michael Davidson, p. 274. New York: New Directions, 2002.

———. ["Interview with L. S. Dembo."] *Contemporary Literature* 10 (Spring 1969): 159–77.

———. "Of Being Numerous." In *New Collected Poems,* edited by Michael Davidson, pp. 163–88. New York: New Directions, 2002.

Palmer, Michael. "Idem 4." In *First Figure,* pp. 33–34. San Francisco: North Point, 1984.

Pinsky, Robert. *The Sounds of Poetry: A Brief Guide.* New York: Farrar, Straus and Giroux, 1998.

Pound, Ezra. "Canto VII." In *The Cantos,* pp. 24–27. New York: New Directions, 1975.

———. "Harold Monro." *Criterion* 11 (July 1932): 581–92.

———. "Hugh Selwyn Mauberley." In *Personae: The Shorter Poems,* edited by Lea Baechler and A. Walton Litz, pp. 183–202. New York: New Directions, 1990.

Shakespeare, William. *The History of King Lear: The Quarto Text.* In *The Norton Shakespeare,* edited by Stephen Greenblatt et al., pp. 2318–472. New York: Norton, 1997.

———. *The Tragedy of King Lear: The Folio Text.* In *The Norton Shakespeare,* edited by Stephen Greenblatt et al., pp. 2319–473. New York: Norton, 1997.

Thompson, John. *The Founding of English Metre.* London: Routledge and Kegan Paul, 1961.

Voigt, Ellen Bryant. "Syntax: Rhythm of Thought, Rhythm of Song." *Kenyon Review* 25 (Winter 2003): 144–63.

Whitman, Walt. "Song of Myself." In *Complete Poetry and Collected Prose,* edited by Justin Kaplan, pp. 188–247. New York: Library of America, 1982.

Williams, William Carlos. *Kora in Hell.* In *Imaginations,* edited by Webster Schott, pp. 6–82. New York: New Directions, 1970.

———. "Pastoral." In *The Collected Poems. Vol. 1, 1909–1939,* edited by A. Walton Litz and Christopher MacGowan, pp. 42–43. New York: New Directions, 1986.

———. *Spring and All.* In *The Collected Poems. Vol. 1, 1909–1939,* edited by Walton Litz and Christopher MacGowan, pp. 177–236. New York: New Directions, 1986.

———. "To a Poor Old Woman." In *The Collected Poems. Vol. 1, 1909–1939,* edited by A. Walton Litz and Christopher MacGowan, p. 383. New York: New Directions, 1986.

Wright, C. D. "Various Positions." In *Steal Away: Selected and New Poems*, p. 161. Port Townsend, WA: Copper Canyon Press, 2002.

Wright, James. "Lying in a Hammock at William Duffy's Farm in Pine Island, Minnesota." In *Above the River: The Complete Poems*, p. 122. New York: Farrar, Straus and Giroux, 1990.

Yeats, W. B. "The Fascination of What's Difficult." In *The Poems*, edited by Richard J. Finneran, p. 93. New York: Macmillan, 1989.

———. "Journal." In *Memoirs*, edited by Denis Donoghue, pp. 137–278. New York: Macmillan, 1973.

———. "Upon a House Shaken by the Land Agitation." In *The Poems*, edited by Richard J. Finneran, pp. 95–96. New York: Macmillan, 1989.

JAMES LONGENBACH (1959–2022) was the author of six books of poetry, including *Forever* and *Earthling*, a finalist for the National Book Critics Circle Award. He was a celebrated critic and author of nine books on poetry, including *The Lyric Now*, *How Poems Get Made*, and *The Virtues of Poetry*. He received an Award in Literature from the American Academy of Arts and Letters and taught for many years at the University of Rochester.

The text of *The Art of the Poetic Line* is set in Warnock Pro, a typeface designed by Robert Slimbach for Adobe Systems in 2000. Book design by Wendy Holdman. Composition by Prism Publishing Center. Manufactured by Versa Press on acid-free paper.